URBAN ECONOMICS

David W. Rasmussen
Florida State University

Harper & Row, Publishers
New York, Evanston, San Francisco, London

Urban Economics

CONTENTS

PREFACE

The field of urban economics is still in its infancy. Although the body of knowledge concerning cities is expanding at a most impressive rate, the development of this specialty within the discipline of economics has been uneven. Most of the scholars interested in the subject have concentrated on problems of regional growth and development. Until very recently the typical book on "urban economics" has focused on such problems, with only a few chapters devoted to such questions as central city decay and the urban public sector. Urban rioting and increased concern over pollution and congestion during the late 1960s have led many economists to consider the economy of cities in greater detail. Crisis conditions facing our major cities have created a surge of interest in urban economics.

It is my conviction that the state of knowledge about the urban economy is not yet sufficient to support a comprehensive textbook summarizing a growing accumulation of technical literature. This volume is designed to provide an overview of the subject for undergraduates in urban economics and graduate students in other disciplines. The book summarizes the basic issues in the field and presents a framework for analyzing urban economic problems. A companion volume, *The Modern City: Readings in Urban Economics*, edited by the author and Charles T. Haworth, is also available.

Many of my colleagues have contributed to the writing of this book. Chapter 9 is based on research conducted with Charles T. Haworth, and much of that chapter is the product of our joint efforts. David

Greytak, William E. Laird, William K. Tabb, and Samuel E. Vichness reviewed the manuscript in its various stages and made many valuable comments. A. Thorvaldson provided useful assistance throughout the book's preparation.

1
THE URBAN CRISIS

Throughout the history of man, both cultural and economic progress have flourished in cities. Man's highest achievements have been realized in urban areas, where the greater degree of personal and political freedom favored the full development of individual ability and initiative. Although the city has traditionally been considered a center of intellectual and cultural activity, the modern city in America is in a state of crisis. Poverty, blight, congestion, pollution, and crime are among the problems that concern the millions living in metropolitan areas. Many Americans, far from viewing our cities as sources of pleasure and enlightenment, seek to escape the problems of urban life.

Many problems facing industrialized urban societies such as ours are not new; the history of the industrial age contains ample documentation of their existence. Poverty, disease, and poor housing have long been familiar conditions to residents of cities. Much of what is perceived as the urban crisis in America is the failure of this country to realize the potential offered by its affluence. Problems associated with the creation of a high-quality urban environment in this nation constitute a frontier for which many public policies of the past are inappropriate, and new policies are only beginning to emerge. The purpose of this volume is to discuss the more important economic problems that are related to the urban crisis in America and to explore policy alternatives for their solution.

1

THE EXTENT OF URBANIZATION

Urbanization is a product of industrial society and is based on rising agricultural production that frees labor for manufacturing and service activity in the cities. The farm population required to feed the growing U.S. population has declined for many years. Ten million people lived on farms in 1969, a figure one-third the size of the 1920 farm population. Dramatic increases in urbanization have accompanied the rising productivity of farm workers. At the time of the first census in 1790, only 6 percent of the nation's population lived in urban places with more than 2,500 people. The urban population rose to almost 40 percent of the total at the turn of this century and to 74 percent by 1970. The rapid urbanization of America in the last 100 years is shown in Table 1.1.

Most of the urban population live in relatively large concentrations of people called Standard Metropolitan Statistical Areas (SMSAs). The U.S. Census Bureau defines a standard metropolitan area as a city of 50,000 inhabitants (or two adjacent cities of that size) and the county in which the city is located. All adjacent counties sufficiently integrated socially and economically with the county of the central city are also included in the metropolitan area. Hence it is possible for one metropolitan area to be made up of counties from more than one state. In this book the terms "urban area" and "city" are used to mean metropolitan area. The principal city of an urban area is called the "core city" or "central city."

The United States has become a nation of cities. The solution to urban problems thus takes on added urgency because our national

TABLE 1.1 Growth in number and population of larger U.S. urbanized areas (500,-000 population and over), 1850–1970

Year	Number of larger urbanized areas	Total population (millions)	Percentage of U.S. population
1850	1	0.7	3
1860	2	1.6	5
1880	3	3.6	7
1900	7	11.0	15
1920	15	23.9	23
1940	19	36.6	28
1960ᵃ	37	65.9	37
1970	42	85.0	42

ᵃ Alaska and Hawaii admitted as states in 1959; included in U.S. totals since then.
SOURCE: Jerome P. Pickard, Office of the Deputy Undersecretary, U.S. Department of Housing and Urban Development, "Growth of Urbanized Population in the United States: Past, Present and Future." (Presented at Conference on the National Archives and Urban Research, Washington, D.C., June 18, 1970).

well-being is closely related to the fate of our cities. If present trends continue and there is no major reduction in the rate of population growth, a burgeoning of our already large cities will occur in the next 30 years. According to a forecast made by the U.S. Census Bureau in 1970, the population of the United States is likely to increase by some 90 million people between 1970 and the year 2000. If all these people were to become urban dwellers, this increase would be the equivalent of creating 8 more metropolitan areas the size of New York in 1967. Allowing for the possibility that some readers think New York is too large, we could instead create 20 new places the size of the Detroit metropolitan area, or 37 the size of Saint Louis in the same year. Assuming no dramatic steps are taken to control or disperse population in the next three decades, it seems likely that the urban crisis is still in its infancy.

The increased urbanization that the United States is likely to experience in the next few decades may result in a dramatic increase in our largest and most densely populated cities. Already in 1970, 11 percent of the nation's population lived in urban areas with an average population density exceeding 10,000 per square mile. In New York City each of the 1.6 million residents of Manhattan shares a square mile of the borough with more than 74,000 other persons. The high population density that characterizes many large metropolitan areas can lead to an intense use of both air and water resources, contributing to their pollution. Because these problems pose a threat to human existence, they take on added urgency. Furthermore, high-density living also yields congestion of public transportation and recreation facilities. The size and density of our major metropolitan areas suggest that concern over the urban condition is not likely to be a quickly passing phenomenon.

THE NATURE OF THE URBAN CRISIS

The awareness of an urban crisis in the past decade is paradoxical in view of the fact that Americans, by many measures, have never been better off. In recent years, when the residents of urban America have become richer, better housed, better educated, and healthier than ever before, disenchantment with urban life has increased. This paradox of rising material well-being coinciding with increasing concern for the future of our urban society can be explained in two ways.

In the first view, the source of the modern urban crisis lies not in the absolute failure of our cities, but rather in the low level of urban life relative to the high-quality environment the nation could realize, given its tremendous resources and wealth. Low incomes, poor housing, and unrest, for example, have been common sights in urban America, but in the past they represented the poverty of the nation. This previous "majority poverty" and the conditions it fostered were facts of life, parameters of the socioeconomic system that could not be changed in the short run. In the post–World War II era, however, the poverty that causes slums and urban riots remains a problem for a steadily declining portion of the population. Unlike majority poverty, poverty confined to a relatively small number of people can weigh on the conscience of the nation, because policy can influence this condition and reduce the accompanying urban ills. Rising affluence in America may be generating the increased concern over urban problems—not because they are worse than they have been in the past but because our ability to improve the quality of urban life has increased. This view led Edward Banfield to claim that most urban problems are "important in the sense that a bad cold is important, but they are not serious in the sense that a cancer is serious."[1]

The above explanation for the increased concern about urban problems is essentially an economic one; it claims that as their income rises, people demand better performance from social institutions. Dissatisfaction is the product of expectations rising faster than performance. A second view is basically noneconomic in nature and is so widely held among observers of the modern world that it cannot be taken lightly. In this view, the increasing sense of crisis in urban areas is a product of alienation—a sense of estrangement from one's environment. Some insight into the source of this lack of identification with the environment can come from the description of a modern industrial society: homogeneous labor and the decline of craftsmanship, standardized output, and atomized rather than extended families. The terms homogeneous, standardized, and atomized describe the relation between machines more aptly than interactions between people.[2] Alienation may be the product of a breakdown in the sense of community that people enjoy in less mobile societies but which is thought to interfere with the production of goods and services in a mechanized, modern industrial economy.

Zoologist Desmond Morris argues that while man has evolved to live in small groups, he is frequently placed in the stressful situation of having to deal with a larger number of people in metropolitan areas.[3] If a person attempts to assimilate too much incoming information, he may suffer from "input overload," which can result in a breakdown of the individual. To defend themselves against the onslaught of humanity in large cities, people set up "an incredibly complicated series of interlocking and overlapping tribal groups." People identify with members of these subgroups and repress their natural tendency to relate to others. This source of estrangement of people in cities is not caused by industrialization per se but rather by large concentrations of population. Alienation of this form may in part explain why city dwellers often watch people being robbed and beaten without intervening on the victims' behalf.

The sense of crisis that surrounds our cities may be related to basic tensions caused by the large-scale, machine-dominated society. John Friedman has suggested that continued urban economic growth will result in an urban culture that is a "thoroughly organized, impersonal and functionally rational society."[4] Ezra Mishan has argued that ". . . wherever people lived comfortably, whether in town or village, or farm, their satisfactions were rooted ultimately in their closeness to each other and to the natural order of their lives."[5] If Mishan is correct in his view of the conditions necessary for the good life, three sources of alienation emerge from the organization of modern society.

The mobility of the population is one source of alienation. Each year over 6 percent of the U.S. population moves from one county to another. This geographic mobility weakens family ties and reduces many personal friendships to a series of transitory relations. The stable neighborhood that characterized major portions of cities in the past has been weakened as a result of this mobility. Free and meaningful contact between neighbors is reduced by the lack of neighborhood identity, a problem aggravated by the rising crime rate in the central city. Escape to the suburb does little to reestablish the lost sense of community. The distance between dwellings in these low-density residential developments discourages contact between neighbors, a source of estrangement reinforced by the automobile, which allows people to identify with citywide subgroups rather than people living nearby.

A second source of alienation in a modern city is the nature of work in industrial society. Mass production techniques have caused a decline in the craftsmanship that has long been a source of reward from work.

The plain truth is that factory work is degrading. It is degrading to any man who ever dreams of doing something worthwhile with his life; and it is about time we faced the fact. The more a man is exposed to middle class values, the more sophisticated he becomes and the more production-line work is degrading to him. . . . Almost without exception, the men with whom I worked on the assembly line last year felt like trapped animals. Depending on their age and personal circumstances, they were either resigned to their fate, furiously angry at *themselves* for what they were doing, or were desperately hunting other work that would pay as well and in addition offer some variety, some prospect of change and betterment.[6]

Unfortunately, white-collar work, with its routinized busywork and paper shuffling, does not provide a reliable refuge from this drudgery.

Dissatisfaction with urban life may in part be a result of the nature of work that is a product of mass industrialization.

Mishan's contention that the good life is based on "natural order" suggests that estrangement from nature is a third source of alienation in urban society. For residents of the largest metropolitan areas, recreational sites in natural settings are increasingly crowded, expensive, and distant. Pollution fouls potential urban sites for water recreation, while air pollution threatens the remaining vegetation in some cities. Observing life from a totally man-made metropolis, urbanites lose sight of their dependence on nature while immersing themselves in the artificially fast pace of the city. This isolation of modern man from his fellows, his work, and nature may be the basis for the alienation that some observers feel is at the root of the urban crisis in America.

Questions relating to the quality of life are inherent in both the rising-affluence interpretation and the alienation interpretation of the urban crisis. In an affluent society such as ours, the intense biological needs for food and shelter are satisfied, thus depriving people of a basic sense of mission—physical survival. The demise of such an elemental goal raises more difficult problems relating to the spiritual needs of man—issues that go beyond the domain of the economist. In this context, the task of the urban economist is to study physical and social aspects of city life that affect the ability of the populace to achieve these higher goals.

URBAN PROBLEMS OR NATIONAL FAILURES?

Because a great many problems facing America occur in metropolitan areas, it is frequently assumed that their solution is to be found in the city. However, the presence of a problem in an organism does not imply that the difficulty can be solved by the efforts of that entity. A sick person does not generally attempt to cure himself—he goes to a doctor. The solution lies not in the person with the problem but rather with a professional who may have the necessary tools and skills. Similarly, there is no reason to assume that the city can solve all the problems that exist within its borders. For the purposes of elaborating public policy, it is important to determine what level of government can most effectively deal with the problem at issue. Of course, if given no alternative, the city must attempt to deal with the issues with all the tools at its disposal, however meager they may be.

Some urban problems can be viewed as a product of national failures rather than as a breakdown in the effective operation of our metropolitan areas. In some cases government inaction is the culprit, while in others, federal programs aggravate the problems of the city. Poverty is at the root of many problems in our cities and can best be remedied by policy action at the federal level. A large number of the sick, the aged, and women who head a household of children are poor; by virtue of their physical condition, age, or responsibilities for raising children, they cannot earn an adequate income. Such poverty can be remedied only by transfer payments, e.g., giving the aged sufficient money to live comfortably in their waning years. The governmental units within metropolitan areas are unable to deal effectively with this problem for two reasons. First, because of the structure of governmental responsibility, metropolitan areas do not have the progressive tax base that is required to finance broad-scale transfer payments. More importantly, significant programs operated by local government to relieve poverty are likely to attract the poor from other areas. The mobility of the population means that some areas may fight poverty by encouraging its poor citizens to migrate to more progressive metropolitan areas. Only with a federal program is it likely that the citizens of each city and region of the country will pay their fair share of relieving the burden of the poor who are unable to work.

A necessary condition for fighting poverty among those who are able to work is the maintenance of high levels of aggregate economic perform-ance—a high growth rate in gross national product and low unemploy-ment rates. Only the federal government has the monetary and fiscal tools to affect national economic performance. The federal gov-ernment's national scope and its ability to manipulate aggregate eco-nomic performance enable it to improve the plight of the poor more effectively than can local governmental units. A more complete analysis of the problems of urban poverty are presented in Chapters 3 and 4.

Local governments are not absolved from responsibility because of shortcomings in the performance of the federal government. Fragmen-tation of many metropolitan areas into hundreds of political jurisdic-tions makes it virtually impossible to administer the metropolitan region effectively. Chicago, the most fragmented of the metropolitan areas, is carved into 1,113 separate governmental units. This balkanization frustrates the development of coherent plans for the entire metropoli-tan area and aggravates inequalities within the region. Upper- and mid-dle-income families can move to the suburbs and avoid the tax burdens associated with the aging central city and the poor who live there. The segregation by income class made possible by the multitude of political jurisdictions intensifies the decay of the central city.

The effectiveness of local government can be enhanced if fragmenta-tion is eliminated. Nashville, Tennessee, and Jacksonville, Florida, have consolidated their local governments, thus indicating that the problem of fiscal fragmentation can be corrected locally. While consolidation of the multitude of political jurisdictions is not a panacea, it is an important step that local government can take to increase its effectiveness.

Traffic congestion is another urban problem that must be solved through the initiative of the metropolitan governments. Many of the costly improvements in urban transportation are financed by the federal government as a result of the distribution of tax revenues. However, these federally assisted efforts are essentially local in nature: plans to reduce traffic congestion in Chicago have little or no impact on similar conditions in Los Angeles. Local governments develop transportation plans that are unique to their area, taking into account the social and physical needs of the city as well as its geographic constraints. Unlike the poverty problem, shortcomings in urban transportation can be remedied by efforts unique to each metropolitan area.

Many problems associated with the urban crisis in America are amenable to solution by public policy. Understanding the nature of the problems and the sources of their solutions is a prerequisite for effective public policy. The unique roles of the federal and local governments in meeting the urban crisis can be clarified when this is accomplished. To the extent that dissatisfaction with urban life is a product of alienation caused by industrial society, the task of public policy is made immeasurably more difficult.

NOTES

[1] Edward Banfield, *The Unheavenly City* (Boston: Little, Brown, 1968), p. 6.

[2] For a good discussion of alienation in modern industrial society, see Erich Fromm, *Man for Himself* (New York: Holt, Rinehart & Winston, 1947).

[3] Desmond Morris, *The Naked Ape* (New York: McGraw-Hill, 1967), ch. 6.

[4] John Friedman, "Cities in Social Transformation," *Comparative Studies in Society and History* 4 (November 1961):103

[5] Ezra J. Mishan, *The Costs of Economic Growth* (New York: Praeger, 1967), p. 124.

[6] Harvey Swados, "The Myth of the Happy Worker," in R. Perrucci and M. Pilisuk, eds., *The Triple Revolution: Social Problems in Depth* (Boston: Little, Brown, 1968), p. 238.

2
ECONOMIC THEORY
AND THE SCOPE
OF URBAN ECONOMICS

Unlike the traditional fields of study in economics, such as public finance and international trade, the domain of urban economics is not well defined. This is in part due to the fact that the assumptions of neoclassical price theory postulate a frictionless world in which all persons possess perfect mobility and knowledge. It is also assumed that economic activity does not have any adverse side effects. A model of this kind does not raise issues associated with a spatial unit such as the city—it assumes them away.

A more important reason for the relative neglect of urban economics is that economists have until recently been preoccupied with questions related to increasing the level of national output. Ever since the appearance of Adam Smith's *The Wealth of Nations* in 1776, economists have struggled to learn how people could enjoy a higher standard of living. Industrialization raised national output but was accompanied by the business cycle. Economists turned en masse to solve this problem when the Great Depression of the 1930s dramatized the instability of a modern economy. John Maynard Keynes's *General Theory* (1936) provided a framework that improved the government's ability to stabilize the economy. The relative stability of the U.S. economy in the post–World War II era testifies to the success of this work.

Rising affluence and relative economic stability have led many economists to analyze other social problems. In the decade of the sixties, poverty, the economics of discrimination, and urban and regional problems received much attention from economists. The purpose of this chapter is to define the scope of urban economics and to identify its role among the many fields of study within the discipline. Before turning to this task, a brief summary of the basic tenets of economic theory is presented.

THE ECONOMICS PERSPECTIVE: EXTERNALITIES

Urban areas are complex societies in which each person is dependent on many other persons for economic and social services. Several "urban theorists" have argued that the purpose of the city is to foster this interdependence which increases economic efficiency and social advancement. Contact with a wide variety of people, products, and points of view is seen as a source of culture and experience that transcends the drudgery and struggle typical of the historical rural existence. For economists this interdependence creates a division of labor that develops the markets for commodities and services, which provide the subject matter of the discipline. Inasmuch as economics is the study of markets, it is to a large extent a product of modern industrial, and hence urban, society.[1] Ironically, the interdependence that characterizes urban life and economic theory also yields "externalities," one of the most serous theoretical problems facing the discipline. Externalities are effects of economic actions that affect parties not directly involved in the transaction. A net external economy occurs if the external economies resulting from a transaction exceed the diseconomies.[2] If, for example, the expansion of manufacturing activity in a city brings about improved business services for all firms, an external economy of scale has benefited the original establishments in the area, even though they paid nothing for the improved services. On the other hand, an external diseconomy occurs if an activity imposes more costs than benefits on society. If a business establishment pollutes the air, it may lower the welfare of citizens in the surrounding area as well as raise the costs of production for firms that require clean air. These negative externalities may be as serious as life-threatening air and water pollution or as trivial as the irritation to a person who happens to sit next to a smoker in a taxi or bus.

   The interdependence that gives relevance to the classical economic theory also contains the root of its most fundamental shortcoming. Taken all together, these externalities may have become sufficiently important to outweigh the advantages that the uncontrolled market mechanism offers its participants. The large volume of advertising by major corporations emphasizing their efforts to curb pollution in recent years is a clear indication that few in modern America are willing to defend the sanctity of a laissez-faire economy to the exclusion of its external effects.

Although externalities have not yet been well integrated into traditional theories of resource allocation, economists are increasingly aware of potential third-party effects that render the "free market" allocation of resources suboptimal. The external effects that have important consequences in urban areas are legion and occur in every problem area that is considered in this volume. However, because the elimination of undesired external effects involves a cost, their presence does not necessarily suggest the need for their reduction or elimination. For example, in a few cases the detrimental effects of pollution may not be sufficient to justify the cost of corrective action. Society need amend the market allocation of resources to include third-party effects only if the benefits of such action exceed the costs.

THE PRINCIPLE OF SUBSTITUTION

Economics is traditionally concerned with the allocation of scarce resources among a number of competing demands. In a basic sense economic theory deals with the theory of choice. The construction of this theory of choice is based on the notion that during a given period of time, each additional unit of consumption or effort in production will yield a smaller incremental benefit than the unit preceding it. For example, the first cold drink consumed on a summer day may be exceedingly enjoyable, while each succeeding one adds increasingly smaller increments of pleasure, until the consumer demands no more. This is generally referred to as the "law of diminishing marginal utility," where marginal utility refers to the change in total pleasure received from an additional unit of consumption. The parallel concept applied to production is the "law of diminishing returns."

These two laws of diminishing effectiveness imply that it may be possible to increase welfare by substituting one activity for another. Thus if the expenditure of an additional dollar on housing will yield more satisfaction than the last dollar spent on food, we may conclude that the consumer would be better off by transferring some of his expenditures from food to housing. This suggests that the much quoted economic adage "more of any good is preferred to less" is often a misleading policy rule because it deals with the wrong question. When faced with limited resources during a specific time period, it may be impossible or undesirable to get more of all goods; the goal to be achieved is the production and/or consumption of the best possible mix of goods, given the level of potential output.

This notion of diminishing effectiveness and substitutability has a great deal of relevance for urban problems. Much criticism has been aimed at the inadequate level of public services in our major metropolitan areas. It is frequently argued that public servants, notably policemen and firemen, are underpaid, while many low-income neighborhoods have a grossly inadequate schedule of garbage collection, making large portions of major cities both unsafe and unhealthy. Inadequate waste-disposal systems cause metropolitan areas to dump large quantities of partially treated or raw sewerage into rivers and lakes, making local government one of the most flagrant polluters of our water resources. A dearth of public recreation facilities rounds out the list of inadequate public goods—goods and services that are not rationed by the price system and are therefore shared by all citizens regardless of their level of income. The indigence of the public sector contrasts sharply with the relative abundance of private wealth, suggesting that society might benefit by substituting public goods consumption for that of private goods. This is the essential theme of John Kenneth Galbraith's *The Affluent Society*. The American public appears to have a strong preference for the consumption of private goods, such as additional television sets, automobiles, and electronic gadgets, over the less tangible yet crucial collective goods of high quality education, public health, and safety. It is a basic tenet of economic thinking, the principle of substitution, that provides the theoretical basis for the analysis of this important shortcoming in modern urban life.

OPPORTUNITY COST

A second important premise that dominates the economic approach to social phenomena is the concept of cost. When faced with the question of how much a project or item costs, the typical response is couched in terms of dollars. Thus a new rapid-transit system may cost $100 million. The economist's approach to cost, on the other hand, attempts to pierce this "veil of money," because dollars do not represent the expenditure of real resources—land, labor, and capital. To the economist the cost of any plan of action, be it in production or consumption, is what is sacrificed in order to accomplish that action. The creation of a rapid transit system implies more than the expenditure of $100 million. The cost of such a project is the best alternative use of the resources. For example, $100 million could buy 10,000 units of housing for the poor, a color television for each of 250,000 households, or a new compact automobile for 50,000 people that may negate the need for the rapid-transit system. These housing units, automobiles, or television sets are the cost of the proposed transportation system because they are mutually exclusive events: If society allocates its resources to any one of the four uses, the other three can no longer be achieved because the resources are already spent. This approach to the concept of cost relies on the premise that the best alternative opportunity represents the cost of any expenditure of real resources and is referred to as "opportunity cost."

The concept of opportunity cost has one important implication for past decisions that cannot be changed. Assume, for example, that society has constructed a network of roads that no longer satisfies the needs of an increasingly mobile population. Once a resource is used and is not available for alternative uses, its opportunity cost is zero. A common solution to this problem is to consider the existing system of roads and conclude it must be expanded to accommodate the rising demands for travel. This approach exemplifies what may be called the "tyranny of small decisions," because today's choices are determined by the decisions made yesterday. The economist's approach to cost insists that the creation of roads in the past may have no bearing on the future, because the resources used in their construction are irretrievably lost. Inasmuch as the resources are consumed, their opportunity cost is zero; hence there is no reason to consider them in the discussion of how to satisfy the ever expanding demand for travel. Water over the dam is gone—sunk costs are no longer costs. This means that the costs and benefits associated with expanding the roadway are compared with alternative methods of meeting the increased travel demands, and the most efficient plan should be adopted.

THE ROLE OF TIME IN ECONOMIC DECISIONS

The total consequences of any economic action are usually realized only after the passage of a considerable length of time. The benefits of an automobile are likely to be spread over a five- or ten-year period, those of houses last several decades, while the useful life of a dam is likely to be well over a century. Because some expenditures may yield moderate benefits immediately while others may give very large benefits at some future date, the theory of choice must offer a way to evaluate alternative resource allocations when the benefits vary over time. This problem deals with the issue of time preference or the degree of shortsightedness governing the person or group charged with decision making.[3] Economists generally assume human beings to be myopic, i.e., they prefer present to future gratification of desires. The degree of myopia is measured by the "discount rate." The discount rate is very similar to the concept of interest that is given on savings in bank accounts. The discount rate is the premium a decision maker is willing to pay in order to have present rather than future consumption. If a person or group considers that receiving $1.00 immediately is as acceptable as receiving $1.10 one year later, we may say a discount rate of 10 percent is being employed.[4] A relatively myopic decision-maker may operate with a discount rate of 50 percent, i.e., be willing to accept $0.67 today in place of $1.00 a year from now. Thus a higher discount rate reflects more acute shortsightedness on the part of the decision maker.

Like individuals, societies must evaluate and choose between courses of action with benefits that are spread unevenly over a period of time. This evaluation is based on the social discount rate, a concept usually more implicit than explicit in the decision-making process. The historical course of economic development in the United States has been characterized by the extensive use of natural resources with little concern for their conservation. In earlier years this myopic development strategy made a good deal of sense because of the urgency of present demands in a society that had not satisfied the basic human needs of food, clothing, and shelter. Furthermore, because of the great natural resources of North America, this use of resources in the pursuit of material well-being did not seriously threaten long-run prospects for prosperity. Unfortunately, rising affluence has not greatly diminished our willingness to mortgage the future for the sake of current consumption. This tradition of impatience and shortsightedness is in no small way responsible for our continued acquiescence to the dumping of waste materials in our water resources and atmosphere rather than constructing pollution-free facilities. It is also partly responsible for the leisurely pace at which new pollution-control technology is developed.

Industrialization and economic growth, of course, need not result in the pollution of the environment. The primary culprit is not industrialization per se but rather an implicit high social-discount rate that leads us to value present output far more highly than future benefits. The private corporation is an institution that is rightly dedicated to the goal of satisfying current needs of the population with hopes of realizing a profit for providing that service. In a free enterprise economy, this is the purpose of the private business firm. Because the private corporation is interested in current profit, it is often a shortsighted institution that cannot effectively deal with phenomena likely to affect the quality of life for society at large 25 years hence. In satisfying current needs, business firms have often lowered their waste disposal costs and raised profits by discharging their refuse into "free" air and water resources. While performing their legitimate function, business firms have contributed to the pollution of the environment.

Since private enterprise is oriented more to the present than to the future, another institution must protect future generations from the myopia of private business decision-makers. Government has the responsibility of being the caretaker of society's long-run interests. Thus the social discount rate employed in public sector decisions *should* be considerably lower than that which governs private decision making. Unfortunately, this role of government is frequently ignored by economists who argue that government should employ a social discount rate equal to that of the private sector.

An important function of government is to regulate private enterprise to ensure that its decisions designed to satisfy short-run desires do not conflict with the broader and more long-run interests of society. The politically popular phrase "bring a business approach to government" negates a basic role to be played by the public sector. Hardheaded business thinking is not likely to place proper emphasis on the long-run projects that may be imperative if we are to achieve an environment of high quality in our urban centers of the future. Decision making in government, as in private enterprise, must be based on a careful calculation of costs and benefits of various decisions. Protection of environmental quality in the urban areas of the future requires that we accept a low discount rate reflecting the long-run interests of society at large, which may conflict with the short-run interests of some private interest groups.

EFFICIENCY AND ECONOMIC GROWTH

These principles of economic thinking—the concepts of substitution, opportunity cost, and time preference—are part of a theory of choice designed to achieve the most efficient allocation of resources. Economic efficiency is often measured in terms of gross national product (GNP): the monetary value of all goods and services produced in the economy during a year. It is assumed that an item's price measures its contribution to national welfare. The inadequacy of using market prices to measure human welfare is easily demonstrated. Water, though very inexpensive, is crucial to human existence, while the more expensive automobile is merely convenience upon which life does not depend.[5] To associate human welfare with the level of GNP is to run the risk of mistaking the price of an item for its value.

This conventional view implies that whatever serves to increase the

GNP or raise its rate of growth is good, while programs and activities that do not contribute to national output are inefficient. A preoccupation with what economist Ezra Mishan has called "growthmania" can result in nebulous gains in social welfare disguised in a wrapping of misleading data. For example, the use of national income accounts (GNP) as a measure of social welfare is clearly fallacious when a $100 million increase in expenditures for war materials is assumed to improve social welfare as much as a similar outlay for new hospital facilities.[6] National income accounts are based on the assumption that a dollar spent on any good or service yields the same utility or satisfaction as a dollar spent on any other item. Thus, the conventional method of quantifying social welfare contradicts a basic tenet of economic theory, i.e., the principle of substitution. When GNP rises with the production of a new car, the possibility that the additional car does not yield as great an increase in satisfaction as a comparable outlay on a new urban sewer-system is totally ignored.

This method of social accounting also confuses negative consequences of production for an output of useful goods and services. In effect, "negative production" or social costs are added to GNP rather than subtracted. When a steel producer sells a ton of steel, the entire value of the output is counted as an economic good, i.e., yielding social benefits. The fact that the production of steel caused many pounds of pollutants to be discharged into the water and air around the plant is ignored. As a result of this pollution, cleaning costs rise, outdoor recreation opportunities are diminished, and the health of some persons living in the area may be threatened. To use market prices as the basis for the measurement of well-being is to ignore the externalities that abound in the modern city. An idling automobile engine on an urban expressway during rush hour does little to improve the welfare of the car's driver and passengers, yet GNP rises with each drop of gasoline consumed during the traffic jam. These examples illustrate the shortcomings associated with the use of GNP accounts as a measure of efficiency. Indeed there is no necessary connection between economic efficiency and the growth of GNP. Efficiency is defined as the ability to choose and use the most effective and least wasteful means of doing a task or accomplishing a purpose. If a society places a high value on leisure and beauty, low levels of production may be more compatible with its goal than high output.

Two basic urban problems are related to the focus on economic growth as the objective of modern social organization. First, it has led to a veneration of the productive citizen and a jaundiced view of the impoverished. This attitude towards poverty has resulted in a general skepticism of programs designed to reduce the incidence of poverty.

Such programs are seen as handouts, and policies are often implemented in such a way that the poor feel dishonorable and unworthy. Granting all possible merit to this skepticism about the motivations of the potentially productive poor, this general attitude reduces the life of the sick and elderly to a degrading existence. Worst of all, children reared in poverty-stricken households are deprived of the cultural background and education required to improve their socioeconomic status in later years. The aura of purity with which working for a living and contributing to economic growth are surrounded results in a gross failure of policy to lighten the burden of people who by virtue of age, health, or family responsibilities are unavoidably unproductive. Some of the problems associated with urban poverty can be solved only with a new specification of national goals. Such a respecification might make it more efficient to achieve the goal of a comfortable life for the aged than to reward some productive workers with a second color-television set.

The chronic impoverishment of the public sector is another urban problem related to the traditional view that economic growth is synonymous with efficiency. Developing a park in a major metropolitan area may provide clear benefits in terms of recreational facilities and the pleasantness of the surrounding area. In a narrow and shortsighted economic perspective, allocating land for such a purpose is inefficient. The traditional view is that such land could be used for industrial, commercial, or residential uses. According to this argument, the public interest has a stake in the private development of the land because it would yield tax revenues that public ownership would deny the city. A city park produces only intangible benefits—those derived from a stroll or a family picnic. These satisfactions cannot be counted in the national income accounts, whereas competing uses of the land raise the measured welfare with a dollar outlay for goods and services. In this sense the traditional narrow and short-run view of efficiency in America, an almost singular appreciation for economic growth, has hindered the development of the public sector and is in part responsible for inadequate public facilities in our major metropolitan areas.

The role of the economist in the analysis of the contemporary urban crisis is to use his discipline's conceptual framework on the relevant issues. These basic principles are few in number yet constitute a relatively powerful tool-kit for the analysis of urban problems. In this volume an economic perspective is used to gain a better understanding of urban phenomena. An attempt will be made, however, to present a broader and longer-run view of economic efficiency than is often encountered. Important limitations that noneconomic factors place on the analysis will also be investigated.

THE CITY AS A FACTOR OF PRODUCTION

Ever since Adam Smith, economists have recognized three factors of production: land, labor, and capital. It is often useful, however, to broaden this view. In its most general sense, the process of production transforms natural resources into items that are useful to man. In this broad sense, any object or organization that fosters this process of creating utility may be referred to as a factor of production. If the city is to be a factor of production, it must be able to raise the welfare of its residents to a level above that which they could enjoy in a nonurban environment. The purpose and justification for the city lies in its ability to create "utility," and the functioning of our urban areas must be evaluated in terms of how well they perform this task. The contribution of cities to the improving of human welfare lies in their ability to perform three basic functions: (1) provide externalities in production; (2) permit economies of scale in consumption; and (3) facilitate upward social mobility.

Externalities in production

Advantages of an urban location accruing to business firms have long been recognized by economists. In fact, the father of modern price theory, Alfred Marshall, argues that they frequently dwarf internal economies of scale:

> . . . we have seen how the economies which result from a high industrial organization often depend only to a small extent on the resources of individual firms. Those *internal* economies which each establishment has to arrange for itself are frequently very small as compared to those *external* economies which result from the general progress of the industrial environment; the situation of a business nearly always plays a great part in determining the extent to which it can avail itself of external economies; and the situation value which a site derives from the growth of a rich and active population close to it, or from the opening up of railways and other good means of communication with existing markets, is the most striking of all the influences which changes in the industrial environment exert on cost of production.[7]

External economies of scale within an industry occur if a decline in average per unit cost for each firm is associated with an expansion of the industry. If an industry expands in a given urban area and results in lowered costs for *only* those firms in the area, the external economy of scale is called immobile. That is, if a firm within the industry moves to another city, it will lose the advantage of agglomeration and, ceteris paribus, will experience a rise in average cost. More generally, however, firms often experience external economies of scale with the expansion of any industry. The reduction in cost per unit produced may result from any one or more of the following "agglomeration economies":

(1) Expansion of economic activity in an area creates additional demand for specialized business services that are performed by auxiliary firms and may increase their availability. This may lower the costs of production in several ways. For example, the proximity of firms specializing in equipment maintenance, of suppliers of sophisticated business machines, and of other technical services allows firms to adopt the most advanced technological devices with little danger of costly breakdowns due to inadequate maintenance or repair. Major financial institutions within the urban area facilitate the borrowing of capital for expansion, particularly for smaller firms without access to the national capital market. In general, the availability of business services facilitates operation with fewer delays in meeting urgent needs.

(2) Metropolitan areas usually offer superior transportation facilities for the movement of required inputs, personnel, and final outputs. Expressways and more frequent rail and air connections can lower the costs of production, particularly for firms that produce commodities sold in national markets.

(3) Large and flexible pools of labor that exist in metropolitan areas also lower the cost of production for many firms. This stock of labor permits firms to lay off and hire workers as they are needed with little danger of being caught shorthanded. This advantage of agglomeration permits the business firm to maintain the optimum size of labor force for profit maximization. From the consumer's point of view, this contribution of reducing the average cost of production is clearly beneficial. However, since many consumers are part of the labor supply that may be hired and fired at will, this advantage of agglomeration may be a mixed blessing from the point of view of the population at large. However, as long as the economy remains reasonably close to full employment, the individual firm has the advantage of flexibility in its labor force while the individual worker is reasonably sure of continuous employment.

(4) Another external economy of scale made possible by the general expansion of industry in urban areas is the reduction of inventory costs. The proximity of suppliers of manufactured inputs reduces the uncertainty of delays in transportation and permits the more frequent delivery of small shipments, thereby reducing the inventory required for continuous production.

In addition to the external economies of scale associated with the expansion of industry, agglomeration may reduce costs of urban services used by the business firm. Modest economies of scale have been found in the production of fire protection, gas, electricity and in sewerage treatment. These economies will lower costs via reduced tax payments and lower utility rates to the private corporation.

Economies of scale in consumption

In addition to facilitating production, concentrations of population can provide consumers with a greater variety of goods and services than do smaller urban centers. Economies of scale in consumption are realized in part because of the large population required to support infre-quently used services. For example, only our largest cities can support professional athletics, theater, opera, and the symphony. Exclusive clothing shops and high-quality restaurants also require the relatively large number of affluent patrons found only in large cities. By virtue of large population, each consumer in a major metropolitan area has an option to consume these infrequently used and often expensive serv-ices. His counterpart in small urban centers, of course, has no such option without the added cost of transportation.

Provision of certain professional services is also facilitated in larger metropolitan areas. A more complete range of medical and dental serv-ices is available in those areas where a large population can support highly specialized medical personnel and equipment. Thus economies of scale in consumption are likely to offer the population in relatively large metropolitan areas a more varied market basket of goods and services.

Metropolitan areas not only provide a wider variety of goods and services, they also provide many commodities more effectively than do small urban centers. In areas with relatively small populations demand for many durable and semidurable goods is sufficiently low for mer-chants to carry only small inventories and few varieties. Consumers are often denied the opportunity to compare alternative brands and fre-quently must purchase a product with inadequate knowledge of the alternatives. In general, residents of relatively small urban places are more likely to face a regional monopolist when purchasing goods and services.

It is frequently assumed that the level of consumer satisfaction is related to the amount of goods and services he consumes and that work is a source of pain or disutility. This is a simplistic view of work, since some individuals have chosen occupations paying less money but offer-ing more interesting and rewarding work. For many individuals, work can be a source of satisfaction. In larger cities the occupational struc-ture is more complete than in smaller towns, offering both primary and secondary workers in households a wider range of jobs with varying skill and time requirements. This large number of occupations offers members of the labor force the opportunity to find employment that suits their needs and desires, thus increasing their welfare over what it would be in a location with fewer options.

The above economies of scale in consumption that are realized in larger cities are economic in nature. They facilitate the consumption of both public and private goods, as well as offering workers a higher probability of finding an occupation with a desirable amount of effort and time expended on the job. Yet another benefit of the city is its relative tolerance to different life styles and divergent ideas. In such an environment the citizen has a greater range in the choice of friends, a particularly important benefit to those who do not accept the prevailing conventional mores and morals. In short, there is a degree of anonymity in the city that gives people an intellectual and personal freedom not always enjoyed in small towns. The city's relatively free environment, coupled with its relatively affluent population, may explain its role as a center of artistic, cultural, and intellectual advance. This freedom is not, however, without cost. It may be argued that too much freedom destroys the sense of community and the individual's sense of identity with both the past and present. The freedom of the city, coupled with a loss of self-identity, may be an important source of the alienation many observers find in modern urban society.

The upgrading function

The upgrading function emphasizes the upward social and economic mobility of the poor. The city is the geographical location where the poorest members of society are most likely to find opportunities to improve their socioeconomic status. Employment opportunities in rural areas are rapidly vanishing, while the number of jobs available in urban areas continues to expand. Furthermore, the large number of job opportunities in metropolitan areas increases the possibility that a worker of any skill level may find employment. This range of employment opportunities also enhances the possibility that, once employed, the worker will be able to improve his economic well-being by moving up the job ladder to a higher-paying occupation. The large variety of jobs also permits secondary wage earners in poor households to enter and leave the labor force at will, as well as offering a wide range of part-time employment opportunities.

In addition to the benefits of the large pool of available jobs, the upgrading function of the city is facilitated by the economies of scale associated with the dissemination of information about employment opportunities. The maintenance of public and private employment agencies becomes possible when a large number of persons are likely to use such a facility. More importantly, the poor become more visible when they are located in urban centers. This increased visibility of the poor may foster a better understanding of their needs and stimulate interest in solving the poverty problem. People are generally more concerned about problems close at hand than more serious problems many miles away. Although the city facilitates the upgrading of the poor, the problem requires that public policies commit money and manpower to the task.

THE SCOPE OF URBAN ECONOMICS

As an area of study within economics, urban economics is not well defined. This is in part true because economists have traditionally focused their energies on the problems relating to economic growth and the stability of economic activity. Economic growth is, of course, of paramount importance when the basic material needs of the society are not met. Economists have felt an increasing confidence in their understanding of the business cycle. From a theoretical point of view, most of the propositions of the "new" economics based on the work of John Maynard Keynes were well elaborated by the early fifties.

Increased understanding of problems of national economic growth led an increasing number of economists to study the geographical distribution of economic activity. These scholars investigated the economic problems of depressed areas, Appalachia being the classic case in point. Analysis of the economic well-being of geographic regions, of course, included that of the cities within regions. Naturally, urban economics became closely allied to regional economics, and the distinction between the two has remained blurred.

It is not surprising that urban economics is not well defined in light of the relatively recent surge of research in the area. Typically, urban economics is defined in terms of economic problems that occur in cities. If it is assumed that all economic activity occurring in the city is "urban economics," this field of study has incredible proportions. In fact, defined this way, urban economics could replace many of the traditional fields of study.

One writer claims that "the urban economy is first a labor market" and that "there is no need to justify discussing unemployment policy under the rubric of urban economics. . . ."[8] With such a broad set of concerns, urban economics is reduced to a reiteration of labor economics and macroeconomic theory. Another author takes the view that economics is a study of markets, and urban economics is concerned with urban markets. The most quantitatively important of these are the markets for residential land and housing.[9] The importance of the labor and housing markets in urban areas is undeniable, yet recognition of this fact does little to clarify the scope of urban economics. This conventional approach suggests there are economic problems that occur most frequently in cities, but there is no unique area of study in the discipline called "urban economics."

If urban economics is a meaningful category of study, it must be defined in such a way that it would analyze important relationships even if the rest of the economy were operating optimally. Do problems of urban economics remain, for example, if there is no unemployment?

Just as the study of technological change will never be obsolete, the field of urban economics, when properly defined, will have a general focus that will survive the problematic concerns of urban areas at the present time. Such a definition is easily derived from the economic advantages of urban life cited above: externalities in production, economies of scale in consumption, and the upgrading function. The study of urban economics deals with how a city affects the economic well-being of its population, i.e., it investigates how cities function as a factor of production. This definition also clarifies the relationship of urban economics to regional economics. Urban economics analyzes how the city raises the welfare of its inhabitants' given levels of population, employment, and per capita income. Regional economics analyzes the forces that determine the geographical distribution of population, income, and employment. This area of study is focused on changes in the location of economic activity and attempts to explain why some cities and regions grow while others decline.

The three ways in which a city ideally increases the welfare of its residents suggest the particular issues that students of urban economics must investigate. Urban poverty falls within the scope of this branch of economics because of the upgrading function. Questions of housing and urban renewal are included because they affect a major portion of consumer expenditures and influence the types of housing available to consumers. Like the physical plant of a private business firm, the city provides spatial organization for microeconomic units. Just as the location of machinery within a plant will influence the efficiency of the firm, so will the location of economic activity within the city influence the utility of its inhabitants. To cite an obvious example, the households in a residential district adjacent to an industrial park that pollutes the air may experience a decline in welfare. An efficient production process in a plant requires that the firm move inputs and outputs from one point to another. Similarly, the city must transport people and materials within its borders. Land use and transportation are thus ingredients in the efficient operation of the city and hence part of the subject matter of urban economics.

It is quite likely that the size of a city will influence the success with which the urban area accomplishes its purposes. Several references have been made to the advantages of larger cities over smaller ones. Yet there is almost certainly a point at which the net advantages of further agglomeration are zero, and negative beyond that. Thus, another area of investigation appropriate for urban economics is the question of optimum city size. Cities also provide microunits in the urban area with public goods such as police and fire protection, education, and other services. The financial needs of the city and its ability to meet these needs are also an integral part of urban economics, since the welfare of urban dwellers is clearly related to the provision of these public services.

These issues constitute the stuff of urban economics. Many of the most important issues of the day are properly part of this area of study within the field of economics. For example, the air pollution crisis in congested areas is closely allied to the widespread use of the private automobile. The chapter on urban transportation sheds light on this problem. In the past, economists have focused on the provision of more goods and services, i.e., economic growth and stability, as the principal vehicle for increases in human welfare while neglecting the external diseconomies so common in cities. To a great extent, urban economics deals with the quality of life, given a level of affluence, rather than focusing an increasing gross national or regional product.

NOTES

[1] It is not surprising that the industrial revolution was already under way when the father of modern economics, Adam Smith, published his *Wealth of Nations* in 1776.

[2] Even though a net external economy is realized by society at large, some individuals may suffer a loss of welfare while others gain. The desirability of the distribution of these positive and negative externalities remains an unresolved issue.

[3] The term *myopia* is often used to suggest a deficiency in a decision maker. For example, Edward Banfield in *The Unheavenly City* defines low-class people as "present oriented" and high-class people as "future oriented." For the economist these terms describe a time horizon determined by the decision maker's tastes and preferences. Classical economic theory assumes that people know how to maximize their utility and thus makes no value judgment with respect to their time preferences.

[4] The net present value *(NPV)* of benefits *(B)* accruing next year is calculated with the formula $NPV = B/(1 + r)$ where r is the discount rate. Thus the net present value of \$1.10 next year discounted at 10 percent is \$1.00. The more general formulation takes into account many years *(n)* of future benefits:

$$NPV = B_1/(1 + r) + B_2/(1 + r)^2 + \ldots + B_n/(1 + r)^n = \sum_{i=1}^{n} B_i/(1 + r)^i.$$

[5] This is, of course, the famous diamond/water paradox. The paradox is explained by the fact that market prices are determined on the basis of marginal utility rather than total utility.

[6] National defense efforts may be our most important expenditures, because they protect all other social and economic activity. This observation, however, does not imply that an increase in defense expenditures raises national welfare. Assume a level of defense expenditures that assures us that no foreign invasion will be successful. A rise in international tensions may make it necessary to spend additional resources to continue the same level of security from foreign invasion. This increase in expenditures may raise gross national product, but it clearly does not raise national welfare because no increase in security is realized.

[7] Alfred Marshall, *Principles of Economics*, 8th ed. (London: Macmillan & Co., 1966), pp. 365–366.

[8] Wilbur Thompson, *Preface to Urban Economics* (Baltimore: Johns Hopkins Press, 1965), p. 203.

[9] Richard F. Muth, "Urban Residential Land and Housing Markets," in H. Perloff and L. Wingo, eds., *Issues in Urban Economics* (Baltimore: Johns Hopkins Press, 1968), p. 285.

RECOMMENDED READING

Dyckman, John. "The Changing Uses of the City," *Daedalus*, Winter 1961, pp. 111–131. Reprinted in D. W. Rasmussen and C. T. Haworth, eds., *The Modern City: A Book of Readings*. New York: Harper & Row, 1973.

Friedman, John. "Cities in Social Transformation," *Comparative Studies in Society and History* 4 (November 1961): 86–103.

Haworth, Joan G. "Externalities and the City," in Rasmussen and Haworth, op. cit.

Mishan, Ezra J. "What Are Spillover Effects," *Technology and Growth: The Price We Pay*. New York: Praeger, 1969, pp. 29–35.

Wilson, James Q. "The War on Cities," *The Public Interest* 3 (Spring 1966): 27–44. Reprinted in Rasmussen and Haworth, op. cit.

3
A PROFILE
OF THE URBAN POOR

It has been argued that the federal government has more effective tools to solve the poverty problem than has local government. Its ability to influence the level of economic activity permits the federal government to keep the demand for unskilled workers relatively high, while its progressive income tax facilitates transfer payments to the poor who cannot work. However, the national government has also aggravated the urban poverty problem with its policies toward rural America. Dramatic increases in the productivity of the agricultural sector have been engineered by the U.S. Department of Agriculture. The rising output per farm workers meant that many of the less productive smaller farms could no longer operate at a profit. Because the federal government made no attempt to develop other jobs in these rural areas, displaced farm workers have been forced to move to the metropolitan areas in search of jobs. This flood of unskilled workers has been too great for the urban economy to absorb into the employed labor force. Thus the poverty problem in urban areas is in part the making of the federal government. Large-scale local government efforts to solve the poverty problem are likely to be frustrated because they would attract more poor people from other areas. Hence the poverty problem in cities may be more a product of national failures than urban mismanagement.

Much of the urban crisis can be linked to the presence of the poor in our relatively affluent metropolitan areas. Poor families cannot pay for adequate housing, and their neighborhoods are often characterized by blight and crime. Decay in the central city encourages middle class families to seek newer housing and more desirable neighbors in the suburbs. Suburbanization of the middle class reduces the tax base of the central city, making it more difficult to arrest its decay. The flight to the low-density suburban areas causes an increased dependence on the private automobile, with its accompanying costs of congestion and air pollution. This scenario suggests that urban poverty is partly responsible for urban sprawl and the decline of the central city into a morass of physical deterioration and crime. Side effects resulting from the increased dependence on the automobile are high levels of congestion and pollution.

This interpretation neglects many other important aspects of the urban crisis, but it does underscore the pervasive influence of poverty on the urban scene. Students of the current urban crisis must therefore understand the nature of poverty and the effectiveness of various proposals for its reduction. This chapter presents a profile of the urban poor and discusses the problems of raising the productivity of workers with low earnings. Chapter 4 analyzes national policies to combat poverty and discusses the urban upgrading function.

WHO ARE THE POOR?

There are two ways to define poverty.[1] The first is based on the premise that people are poor when they have a standard of living below subsistence: the minimum provision of health and working capacity. It may be argued that this is an absolute standard, measurable in such terms as caloric intake and medical care. Alternatively, poverty can be viewed as a relative phenomenon, with the lower end of the income distribution assumed to be in poverty. As the standards and expectations in a society rise as a result of increasing affluence, persons with relatively low and stable incomes may view themselves as being badly off—in some cases, impoverished—in terms of the norms of society. In practice it appears that the United States has adopted this approach because the "official" poverty line has risen faster than the cost of living. A congressional committee in 1949 adopted a $2,000 poverty line for an urban family of four, while the 1962 Council of Economic Advisers used a standard of $3,000. Since the price level rose 32 percent from 1949 to 1962, the latter sum represents an increase in the purchasing power of families at the poverty line.

Despite the fact that poverty is viewed in relative terms in the United States, a case can be made that the income standard is below the subsistence level. The Social Security Administration definition of poverty is based on the U.S. Department of Agriculture "economy food plan," which is designed for "temporary or emergency use when funds are low." This standard suggests that a family of four below the poverty line has an income of less than $3,750 at 1970 prices. Mollie Orshansky describes the adequacy of this level of income:

> Assuming the homemaker is a good manager and has the time and skill to shop wisely, she must prepare nutritious, palatable meals on a budget that for herself, a husband and two young children—an average family—would come to about 88 cents a day per person.
>
> For a meal all four of them ate together, she could spend on the average only $1.15, and to stay within her budget she must allow no more a day than a pound of meat, poultry, or fish altogether, barely enough for one small serving for each family member at one of the three meals. Eggs could fill out her family fare only to a limited degree because the plan allows less than 2 dozen a week for all uses in cooking and at the table, not even one to a person a day. And any food extras, such as milk at school for the children, or the coffee her husband might buy to supplement the lunch he carries to work, have to come out of the same food money or compete with the limited funds available for rent, clothing, medical care, and all other expenses. Studies indicate that, on the average, family members eating a meal away from home spend twice as much as the homemaker would spend for preparing one for them at home. The 25–30 cents allowed for a meal at home in the economy plan would not buy much even in the way of supplementation.[2]

Inadequate income is not the only problem facing poor families. There is considerable evidence that their dollars purchase less than those of their more wealthy counterparts. Food and housing ordinarily account for 60 percent of all consumer expenditures and are the most important areas in which the poor dollar is deflated.[3] David Caplovitz has argued that consumer credit is expensive for the poor. "Society now virtually presents the very poor risks with twin options: of forgoing major purchases or of being exploited." The former is not regarded as a viable alternative because "Americans in all walks of life are trained to consume in order to win the respect of others and to maintain their self-respect."[4]

This tendency to engage in what Thorstein Veblen called "conspicuous consumption" may be strongest in the case of certain minority groups. Caplovitz argues that when the poor have little hope of improving their status, they are likely to engage in "compensatory consumption" to combat the frustration caused by their lack of social mobility. Blacks, Hispanic minorities, and American Indians are the most prominent groups facing discrimination that limits their ability to improve their socioeconomic status.

In 1970 there were 12.3 million persons living in poverty in metropolitan areas. This accounts for 10.3 percent of the metropolitan population. The outstanding feature of the urban poverty profile is that a majority of the poor are not able to improve their economic status.

In 1970 almost 4.7 million children under the age of 15 lived in poor families. In that same year, 2.3 million aged persons lived in poverty. Of over 12.3 million poor persons living in metropolitan areas, 7 million or 57 percent have virtually no control over their situation.

Many able-bodied workers find it difficult to get out of poverty because of discrimination in the labor market. Thirty-one percent of the urban poor are black, a minority that often faces unequal employment opportunities. A large portion of all poor families with children are headed by females. In 1970 women-headed households accounted for 34.5 percent of the poor persons in metropolitan areas. Female heads of household may find it impossible to work full time because of inadequate day-care facilities for their children. Even when employed full time, women often find it difficult to earn a decent income because of the physical requirements of some jobs and frequent discrimination against women in many high-wage occupations.

The profile of poverty in America underscores the importance of distinguishing between the potentially productive and the unproductive poor. Easing the burden of the aged poor can only be accomplished through income transfers to this group. A similar case can be made for families headed by females, although it must be predicated on the continuation of employment discrimination against women and inadequate child day-care centers. Unambiguous examples of the potentially productive poor are males between the prime ages of 18 and 65 and the children living in poor families. Methods of increasing the productivity of these two groups are discussed in the following section.

RAISING THE PRODUCTIVITY OF THE POOR

Many poor families are headed by males who are either unemployed or employed at such a low wage rate that even full-time work does not yield an income above the poverty level. If a person receives an hourly wage of $1.75 and works 40 hours in each of 50 weeks, his earnings would be $3,500—$250 below the poverty line. Economists generally assume that the productivity of a worker is related to the amount of formal education and on-the-job training he acquires. This being the case, the earnings of a worker with a given level of education should generally rise as he gets older and acquires more experience on the job. Also, workers with more formal education in any particular age group will have higher earnings than less educated peers. Table 3.1 shows that this is in fact the case for males up to the age of 54. The decline in earnings for the 55–64 age group may be due to a greater frequency of illness and semiretirement in this higher age bracket. The labor-force

TABLE 3.1 Median earnings of males by age and education, 1970

Age	0–7	8	9–11	12	13–15	16+
			Years of education			
18–24	2,639	3,543	2,744	3,575	2,915	4,571
25–34	5,058	6,078	6,579	7,742	8,261	10,375
35–44	5,572	7,247	7,932	9,193	10,996	16,733
45–54	5,428	7,061	8,172	9,713	12,077	19,213
55–64	4,737	6,437	7,388	8,991	11,282	20,152

SOURCE: Estimated from data available in U.S. Bureau of the Census, *Detailed Characteristics,* PC(1) (Washington, D.C.: Government Printing Office, 1972), Table 197.

participation rate for workers between 55 and 64 is 81.8 percent, while that of the 45–54 group is 93.2 percent.

Formal education increases the earnings of an individual in two ways. The view that permeates traditional economics is that the higher skill level and adaptability of highly educated workers raises their contribution to output and hence they receive higher salaries. There is a second aspect that is particularly important when analyzing poverty. The educational level of employees provides employers with a screening device that separates workers with some intelligence, with habits of punctuality and tenacity, from those who have not *indicated* these traits.

Socializing young persons so that they are adapted to the values and demands of a society is a major function of education, and finishing school signifies completion of this process which prepares people for their role in the productive process.[5] Even though a particular task can be performed equally well by a high school graduate or a dropout, an employer may arbitrarily decide to hire only "good risks," e.g., high school graduates.[6] An individual with a low level of education can be reliable and competent, yet employers may not consider his request for employment because it is assumed he is like most members of this "high risk" group of workers.

The cost of such a hiring policy rises in times of full employment. When the aggregate unemployment rate is low, members of the labor force with little formal education will experience fewer arbitrary barriers to employment than when a large number of workers are seeking employment. James Tobin has argued this position:

In a slack labor market, employers can pick and choose, both in recruiting and in promoting. They exaggerate the skill, education, and experience requirements of their jobs. They use diplomas, or color, or personal histories as convenient screening devices. In a tight market, they are forced to be realistic, to tailor job specifications to the available supply, and to give on-the-job training. They recruit and train applicants whom they would otherwise screen out, and they upgrade employees whom they would in slack times consign to low wage, low skill, and part-time work.[7]

The income profiles presented in Table 3.1 suggest that the principal vehicle by which a person can raise his productivity is to increase the amount of formal education he acquires. Economists generally view education as an investment in "human capital" that yields a stream of benefits in the form of increased income over the working life of the investor. As noted in Chapter 2, economic theory provides a method for analyzing decisions that involve benefits spread over time.

Future benefits are evaluated at less than their face value because of the discount rate—a measure of the preference for present over future consumption. In particular, the net present value (NPV) of an investment in education is:

$$NPV = (\Delta E - C)_1/(1 + r) + (\Delta E - C)_2/(1 + r)^2$$
$$+ \ldots + (\Delta E - C)_n/(1 + r)^n$$

where ΔE is the increase in earnings as a result of the increased schooling and C is the cost of acquiring the schooling including the opportunity cost of forgone earnings. Hence $(\Delta E - C)_i$ is the net benefit of the increased education in year i, and r is the rate at which this benefit stream is discounted.

This framework makes it possible to analyze the position of the poor when faced with the decision of whether or not to increase their productivity by investing in education. Age is clearly an important element in such a decision. Consider a man 55 years of age whose job has been automated out of existence. Going to school would require that he take losses in the early years when ΔE is zero. If the worker is able to find a new job, even very low wage employment will make the opportunity costs of returning to school substantial. After finishing his new training, he has fewer than 10 years of active employment in which to make up the initial losses. This suggests that the payoff to human capital investments made by middle-aged poor workers is liable to be relatively small and that such persons cannot be considered irrational for not furthering their education.

The decision of a high school student from a poor family to remain in school is of more relevance, since over 38 percent of all poor persons are less than 15 years of age. For the moment, let us assume that changes in earnings (ΔE) and the costs of schooling (C) are fixed by the market and institutional setting. With the change in earnings and costs fixed, the one variable that may cause the poor student to drop out of school while his more affluent peer continues is the discount rate (r). Of course, a higher discount rate will discourage investment in education because the value of future benefits is lower.

The law of diminishing effectiveness suggests that the marginal utility derived from present consumption will decline as the quantity increases. This implies that when the more affluent invest in education, they give up current consumption, which gives them a relatively small amount of pleasure. Of course, the wealthier students and their families may not actually sacrifice any current consumption, but merely save a little less than otherwise. Poor families, on the other hand, must sacrifice current pleasures which are highly valued and, in the extreme, may be life sustaining. Investments for increased future consumption are more likely to be undertaken after the intense current needs of food, shelter, and medical care are met. People living close to subsistence are likely to be more present than future oriented. Edward Banfield has argued that this present-orientedness may be a rational adaptation to reality and that some individuals will become future oriented whenever they perceive changes in the situation that make providing for the future profitable.[8]

This present-orientation may reduce the number of poor children in school. Discount rates for different income classes can be estimated from the interest rates they actually face.[9] Estimates of time preference for four income classes are presented in Table 3.2. For the present purpose the relative size of the discount rate by income class is more important than the actual estimates. Families in poverty have a discount rate almost twice that of families with an annual income exceeding $7,500. The impact of this present-orientation on investment decisions is made clear when we consider a net benefit stream of $100 for each of 10 years. For those in the over $7,500 income bracket the net present value of such an increase in earnings is $623 compared to only $403 for those in poverty. Thus the future benefits resulting from investments in education are more highly valued by the wealthy than the poor. The high discount rate of the poor may be a significant factor in reducing the attractiveness of raising future earnings by educational

TABLE 3.2 Discount rates by income level, 1962

Income level	Discount rate
0–3000	9.51
3000–4999	6.78
5000–7499	6.31
over 7500	4.85

SOURCE: D. W. Rasmussen, "Benefit Cost Versus the Rate of Return: An Analysis of Investment Criteria" (Saint Louis: Institute for Urban and Regional Studies, Washington University, October 1966).

investments. This relative myopia is at least in part a product of low income—a fact that helps explain the phrase "vicious cycle of poverty."

A second source of variation between the rich and poor in their willingness to invest in education is the cost of schooling. The concept of opportunity cost suggests that an important component of the cost of education is the consumption forgone while in school. A high school youth from a wealthy family may be furnished with the use of a car, expensive clothing, and vacations to such an extent that to quit school and support himself would actually reduce his level of consumption. In such a case the opportunity cost of acquiring education is zero, or even negative. In contrast the level of consumption realized by a youth from a poverty-stricken family is likely to be so low that his immediate welfare would markedly improve even at the low income that a school dropout can expect to earn. Assuming that a youth in a family of four consumes one-fifth of the household budget, the $2,000 per year a dropout can expect to earn may look attractive to youths from families whose income is near the poverty level but would not tempt those from families with an income of $20,000 a year. In the case of a youth in the latter situation, the cost he personally bears for his education is negative, i.e., the $2,000 income he could earn as a dropout minus the $4,000 he consumes from the family budget. The higher cost of education to the poor, like their relatively high discount rate, is likely to lower the amount of educational investments made by low-income groups.

While the cost of finishing high school is essentially the forgone opportunity of earning income, going to college includes an additional dollar outlay for books and tuition, which raises a further barrier to the poor. Even if the benefits of an educational investment are highly valued by a poor person, he may be unable to pay for the actual momentary costs of continued schooling. As Orshansky's description of the poverty budget suggests, this is likely to be the case for both the poor and the near poor.

The remaining variable in the net present value formulation is the change in earnings (ΔE) that is likely to result from the educational investment. If all persons entering the labor force were homogeneous, it could be argued that the change in earnings was determined by the labor market. However, decisions to invest are not made on what the benefits *will* be, but rather their *expected* level. Some persons are likely to feel they are "losers" and hence view the expected increase in earnings to be very low. Youths from very poor families with no "success models" to emulate are more likely to hold this view than the children of high-achieving white-collar workers. Low expectations may be reinforced if early school years are not particularly successful because inadequate nutrition, medical care or a poor home environment hinder performance. For older workers contemplating a training program, a history of dead ends is likely to generate a similar kind of phenomenon. A history of failure is likely to lower the expected value of benefits from formal education or vocational training. Either real or imagined discrimination may likewise influence the perceptions of minority groups. In each case, the expected economic benefits from educational investments are likely to be lower for the poor than for their wealthy peers.

This tendency to expect small increases in earnings can be confused with an excessive shortsightedness. Elliot Liebow makes this distinction in his study of black street-corner men: "When Richard squanders a week's pay in two days, it is not because, like an animal or child, he is 'present oriented,' unaware of or unconcerned with his future. He does so precisely because he is aware of the future and the hopelessness of it all."[10] To perceive the future and find it wanting is clearly a different phenomenon from the disinterest in the future that characterizes persons with a high preference for current consumption.

The net present value method of evaluating human capital-investment decisions suggests three important variables that influence the anticipated economic payoff of continued schooling. The relatively high cost of education to the poor and the high rate at which they typically discount future benefits are in part *a product of their low income!* The culture of poverty, based on a lack of hope for the future, causes many of the poor to underestimate the returns to be gained from schooling. In the case of these variables that determine the anticipated gains from schooling, expected increase in earnings (ΔE), cost of education (C), and the discount rate (r), the dynamics of being poor are likely to discourage investments in education even when they would be feasible.

The impact of low family income on the willingness of the poor to invest in education suggests an avenue for public policy. The present definition of poverty does not provide a subsistence income and is clearly too low. Concern for poverty in America is based on inadequate current consumption of families. Programs oriented toward such a limited short-run objective are unlikely to foster the appropriate long-run goal of economic independence. A more realistic definition of poverty, coupled with some method of guaranteeing this adequate standard of living to households with children, might remove some of the incentive of poor children to drop out of school. Financial barriers to higher education can be diminished by offering full scholarships or interest-free loans to children from families with low incomes. To alleviate possible work-disincentive effects, partial scholarships should be available to those from families with incomes somewhat over that standard—the dollar value declining as income rises.

The scholastic achievement of children in affluent homes is influenced by their favorable environment, which increases their curiosity and knowledge and gives them a clear advantage over their peers reared in poverty. Seeds of failure are often sown early in life. The importance of early childhood environment suggests the need for programs that attempt to provide a set of preschool experiences for children from deprived backgrounds that is comparable to those of middle class children. Because environmental enrichment continues during the primary and secondary school years, the need for a continuing program for the poor is clear. If the youth in culturally deprived homes today are not to be condemned to a life of poverty, great efforts must be made to improve their educational experience. As to the exact nature of such programs, of course, the educational theorist has more to offer than the economist.

POVERTY AND ECONOMIC GROWTH

Despite few efforts to reduce poverty other than providing subsistence, there has been a dramatic decline in the incidence of economic hardship among families. Economic growth is to be credited for this reduction of poverty in America. Economic growth attacks poverty in two ways. First, a high rate of economic growth means a higher demand for labor relative to supply. Second, an expansion of investment increases worker productivity by increasing both the quantity and quality of the capital stock per worker. The GNP rose from $231.6 billion in 1947 to a 1967 figure of $789.7 billion, an increase of 240 percent. As shown in Table 3.3, the percentage of families with incomes under $5,000 decreased 56 percent during this 20-year period. However, the figures in Table 3.3 probably overestimate the impact of economic growth on poverty. A large part of the rapid growth of output from

TABLE 3.3 Changes in the distribution of family income, 1947–1967 (in 1967 dollars)

Income level	Percent of U.S. population		
	1947	1967	Change
0– 4,999	57.0	25.3	−56
5,000– 9,999	} 34.1	40.3	} 28.6
10,000–14,999		22.4	
over 15,000	8.9	12.0	29

SOURCE: U.S. Bureau of the Census, *Statistical Abstract of the United States, 1969* (Washington, D.C.: Government Printing Office, 1969), p. 323.

1947 to 1967 has been attributed to the higher educational levels of workers in the labor force.[11] To the extent growth is caused by improvements in the quality of labor, poverty has been reduced by education, not by economic growth. The two are related, of course. Nevertheless, it seems clear that economic growth helps reduce the number of people with a subsistence standard of living. Poverty measured in relative terms was largely unaffected by the surge of growth in the post–World War II era. The 20 percent of all families at the bottom of the income distribution received between 4.5 and 5.7 percent of aggregate money income during the fifties and sixties.

Unfortunately, the benefits of economic growth that have filtered down to the poor in the past are not likely to accompany future growth. If the poor are increasingly insulated from the benefits of economic growth, they should similarly be unaffected by cyclical fluctuations in the economy. This is in fact the case. The proportion of the population with incomes of less than $3,000 per year does not change significantly over the business cycle.[12] This is not surprising in light of the fact that almost three-fifths of the poor may be classified as unavoidably "nonproductive," i.e., are not able to work. An increasing proportion of the poor are likely to be in this category as the economy provides employment for the physically fit. Increasing worker productivity and employment opportunities will not reduce poverty among those persons with limited productivity, e.g., children, the aged, the handicapped, and the sick.

Many of the poor in the labor force are unable to find employment even in time of economic expansion because their skills (or lack thereof) are not in demand. Some economists refer to this phenomenon as "structural unemployment," which contrasts to the temporary loss of earnings caused by the changing of jobs by employable workers—called frictional unemployment. Many economists believe that economic expansion will not help many unemployed workers find employment because the jobs created cannot be filled by this "hard core" of unskilled workers. The structuralist position is consistent with the view that technological change is rapidly reducing the demand for unskilled labor. Furthermore, some relatively skilled jobs, as in the mining industry, have been automated out of existence. These skilled workers, many in middle age, must reenter the labor market without marketable skills. If workers are geographically immobile, as many miners are, they face only the local labor markets, which are often depressed because of the decline of the major local industry. Geographic immobility is likely to compound the difficulties of the structurally unemployed worker.

Some economists argue that structural unemployment is not fundamentally different from frictional unemployment. This school of thought claims that workers suffer long periods of unemployment because the demand for labor is too low. This position is based on the assumption that when labor markets are very tight, employers break down complicated tasks into simple ones that even the most unskilled workers can accomplish. These economists argue that the myth of structural unemployment could be destroyed if the rate of growth of economic activity were drastically increased. Superficially, the experience of America during World War II confirms this view.[13]

Citing the traumatic war experience to support the contention that all unemployment is frictional suggests two basic problems with this view. The mobilization for the World War II effort resulted in very high levels of economic activity and worker mobility. The intensity of work effort in those years and the inexhaustible demand created by the war machine may not be achievable except in such periods of national emergency. One would be hard pressed to argue the desirability of an employment policy based on the continuation of crisislike conditions.

A related issue is the widely recognized trade-off between inflation and unemployment: Under our contemporary economic institutions, the cost of low unemployment is a rapidly rising price level. Inflation is a tax on persons living on fixed incomes, such as those receiving only social security payments as well as those with slowly rising incomes. Inflation will also cause an inefficient use of resources if it becomes severe enough to distort the relative price structure. A stable price level is a traditional and widely accepted goal of macroeconomic policy. This inflation-employment trade-off can be estimated by comparing rates of unemployment and inflation over a period of time. One estimate, based on data from the 1933 to 1958 period shown in Figure 3.1, is that a 3 percent unemployment rate results in a 4 to 5 percent rate of inflation, while the price level will not rise when 5.5 percent of the labor force cannot find employment.[14]

The trade-off between employment and inflation suggests that the use of economic growth to counter structural unemployment will be accompanied by inflation. This objection to the use of economic growth to combat structural unemployment has been refuted by major economists in the field of macroeconomic policy. These scholars claim that the trade-off estimated from empirical data does not imply a similar relationship in the future. Milton Friedman has argued that ". . . there is always a temporary trade-off between inflation and unemployment; there is no permanent trade-off. . . ."[15]

Current events confirm that there is no fixed relationship between unemployment and inflation. On the basis of the estimated trade-off

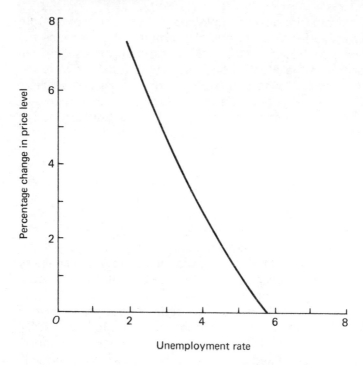

FIGURE 3.1. The Phillips curve: An empirical estimate of the
trade–off between unemployment and inflation,
1933–1958.

SOURCE: P.A. Samuelson and R.M. Solow, "Analytical Aspects of Anti-
Inflation Policy," *American Economic Review,* May 1960,
pp. 177-194.

between 1933 and 1958, the 1969 unemployment rate of 3.5 percent should have been accompanied by a 3.6 percent increase in the
price level. Instead, the cost of living rose 5.5 percent. Economic institutions play a major role in controlling both employment and prices. For
example, the development of acceptable long-term wage and price
controls could make high levels of employment virtually inflation free.
The Phillips curve, shown in Figure 3.1, is not a fixed relationship
between unemployment and inflation. Changes in institutions and expectations can shift the curve to either a more favorable or less favorable trade-off. Unfortunately, a widely held skepticism about wage and
price controls in a free market economy makes it unlikely that the
inflation cost of a low unemployment rate will be substantially reduced.
As a result it is unlikely that low rates of unemployment can be perma-
nently maintained in America, and many able-bodied workers will not

find employment because employers are not forced to utilize unskilled labor.

Many of the potentially productive poor may not enter the labor market for a variety of sociological and psychological reasons. Inasmuch as these factors discourage some of the poor from taking existing opportunities, even the availability of jobs may not benefit this group until their outlook and expectations are improved. Sociologist Elliot Liebow vividly described this failure syndrome among black street-corner men:

> However far he has gone in school, he is illiterate or almost so; however many jobs he has had or hard he has worked, he is essentially unskilled. Armed with models who have failed, convinced of his own worthlessness, illiterate and unskilled, he enters marriage and the job market with the smell of failure all around him. Jobs are only intermittently available. They are almost always menial, sometimes hard, and never pay enough to support a family.
>
> In general, the menial job lies outside the job hierarchy and promises to offer no more tomorrow than it does today. The Negro menial worker remains a menial worker so that, after one or two or three years of marriage and as many children, the man who could not support his family from the very beginning is even less able to support it as time goes on. The longer he works, the longer he is unable to live on what he makes. He has little vested interest in such a job and learns to treat it with the same contempt held for it by the employer and society at large. From his point of view, the job is expendable; from the employer's point of view, he is. For reasons real or imagined, perhaps so slight as to go unnoticed by others, he frequently quits or is fired.[16]

This sense of failure is not unique to blacks nor to modern urban ghettos. Studs Terkel relates a psychiatrist's impressions of white males during the depression:

> I did a little fieldwork among the unemployed miners in Pennsylvania. Just observing. What the lack of a job two, three, four, five years did to their families and to them. They hung around street corners and in groups. They gave each other solace. They were loath to go home because they were indicted, as if it were their fault for being unemployed. A jobless man was a lazy good-for-nothing. The women punished the men for not bringing home the bacon by withholding themselves sexually. By belittling and emasculating the men, undermining their paternal authority, turning to the eldest son. Making the eldest son the man of the family. These men suffered from the depression. They felt despised, they were ashamed of themselves. They cringed, they comforted one another. They avoided home.[17]

Jobs that may be filled by the poor are a necessary but not sufficient condition for the reduction of poverty. Simplistic solutions to minority poverty, such as reliance on economic growth, underestimate the complex psychological and sociological factors that affect the behavior of some potentially productive poor persons. In the next chapter both federal and urban policies to reduce poverty are discussed.

NOTES

[1] See Martin Rein, "Problems in the Definition and Measurement of Poverty," in Louis A. Ferman, et al., eds., *Poverty in America* (Ann Arbor: University of Michigan Press, 1965), pp. 116–131.

[2] Mollie Orshansky, "Counting the Poor: Another Look at the Poverty Profile," *Social Security Bulletin* 28 (January 1965): 10. Expenditure figures are adjusted to 1970 prices.

[3] P. Groom, "Prices in Poor Neighborhoods," *Monthly Labor Review,* October 1966, pp. 1085–1090.

[4] David Caplovitz, *The Poor Pay More* (New York: The Free Press, 1967), p. 180.

[5] See Herbert Gintis, "Repressive Schooling as Productive Schooling," in "New Working Class and Revolutionary Youth," *Socialist Revolution,* May–June 1970. Reprinted in David M. Gordon, ed., *Problems in Political Economy: An Urban Perspective* (Lexington, Mass.: D. C. Heath, 1971).

[6] For a theoretical discussion of this phenomenon, see G. A. Akerhoff, "The Market for 'Lemons': Quality Uncertainty and the Market Mechanism," *Quarterly Journal of Economics* 84 (August 1970): 488–500.

[7] James Tobin, "On Improving the Economic Status of the Negro," *Daedalus,* Fall 1965, pp. 883–884.

[8] Edward Banfield, *The Unheavenly City* (Boston: Little, Brown, 1968), p. 217. Banfield describes two other types of present-orientedness, although there is no necessary connection between being poor and these types of myopia. Cognitive myopia is a psychological inability to take into account the future. The individual with volitional present-orientedness prefers to live from moment to moment—he likes the present-orientation as a life style.

[9] See Otto Eckstein and John V. Krutilla, *Multiple Purpose River Development: Studies in Applied Economic Analysis* (Baltimore: Johns Hopkins Press, 1958), ch. 4. This method is based on the debt-asset position of the population within each income class and the interest rates charged on debts and the rates of return from assets.

[10] Elliot Liebow, *Tally's Corner* (Boston: Little, Brown, 1967), p. 66.

[11] Edward F. Denison, *The Source of Economic Growth in the United States* (New York: Committee for Economic Development, 1962).

[12] Oscar Ornati, "Poverty in Cities," in H. Perloff and L. Wingo, eds. *Issues in Economics* (Baltimore: Johns Hopkins Press, 1968), pp. 345–346.

[13] See Charles Killingsworth, "Jobs and Income for Negroes," in I. Katz and P. Burin, eds. *Race and the Social Sciences* (New York: Basic Books, 1969), pp. 194–274.

[14] P. A. Samuelson and R. M. Solow, "Analytical Aspects of Anti-Inflation Policy," *American Economic Review* 50 (May 1960): 177–194.

[15] M. Friedman, "The Role of Monetary Policy," *American Economic Review* 58 (March 1968):11.

[16] Liebow, op. cit., pp. 211–212.

[17] Studs Terkel, *Hard Times: An Oral History of the Great Depression* (New York: Pantheon, 1970), p. 196.

RECOMMENDED READING

Caplovitz, David. *The Poor Pay More.* New York: The Free Press, 1967.
Jackson, Carolyn and Terri Velter. "Residence, Race and Age of Poor Families in 1966," *Social Security Bulletin,* June 1969. Reprinted in D. W. Rasmussen and C. T. Haworth, eds., *The Modern City: A Book of Readings.* New York: Harper & Row, 1973.
Liebow, Elliot. *Tally's Corner.* Boston: Little, Brown, 1967.
Ornati, Oscar. "Poverty in Cities," in H. Perloff and L. Wingo, eds., *Issues in Urban Econimics.* Baltimore: Johns Hopkins Press, 1968.
Rasmussen, David. "A Note on the Relative Income of Non-White Men, 1948–1964," *The Quarterly Journal of Economics,* February 1970. An updated version of this paper appears in Rasmussen and Haworth, op. cit.
Rein, Martin. "Problems in the Definition and Measurement of Poverty," in Louis A. Ferman, et al., eds., *Poverty in America.* Ann Arbor: University of Michigan Press, 1965, pp. 116–131.
Tobin, James. "On Improving the Economic Status of the Negro," *Daedalus,* Fall 1965.

4
NATIONAL POLICIES
TO COMBAT URBAN POVERTY

Poverty is a complex phenomenon that must be attacked on several different fronts. One of the cornerstones of a viable antipoverty program is the distinction between the potentially productive and the nonproductive poor. The potentially productive poor are those who are able to serve in the labor force, while the nonproductive poor are characterized by their *inability to work.* This is the source of the dilemma confronting efforts to combat poverty. On the one hand, policies must be designed in such a way that the nonproductive poor, such as the ill and aged, are given adequate incomes. On the other hand, it is generally agreed that these programs should not discourage potentially productive poor people from seeking work. Before policies that may help reduce poverty are discussed, current antipoverty programs are analyzed.

SOCIAL WELFARE PROGRAMS IN AMERICA

In 1969 the United States spent about $83.8 billion, or 9 percent of its gross national product, on social welfare programs. Programs that absorbed these expenditures are shown in Table 4.1. Efforts designed to relieve poverty among retired and aged workers and their families account for $48.7 billion, 58 percent of social welfare expenditures. These retirement and insurance programs are designed to assure the average worker that working while he is able (usually up to the age of 65) will be sufficient to support himself and his dependents throughout

TABLE 4.1 Social welfare expenditures, by source of funds, 1969 (in millions of dollars)

Expenditure	Federal	State and local
Old age, survivors, disability and health insurance for aged[a]	33,389	—
Other worker retirement and insurance	7,435	7,896
Veterans and other Defense Department programs	9,821	40
Housing	446	110
Public aid	7,851	5,592
Civilian medical programs	2,790	4,321
Other social welfare	1,903	2,293
Total	63,635	20,252

[a]Under the Social Security Act.
SOURCE: U.S. Bureau of the Census, *Statistical Abstract of the United States, 1970* (Washington, D.C.: Government Printing Office, 1970). p. 277.

their lives. Because these programs are designed to ward off the poverty that may threaten productive workers in the event of disability or retirement, the benefits do not filter down to many of the hard core poor. Female heads of household and their children, unemployed school dropouts, and many occasional workers in low-wage industries are not likely to be recipients of this large sum spent on retirement and worker insurance. The $9.8 billion spent on veterans programs, of course, reach only a limited number of the hard core poverty group.

The nonaged poor who cannot find employment because of a lack of skills, discrimination, or a lack of motivation receive benefits from programs classified as "Public aid" and "Other social welfare" in Table 4.1. These programs include Job Corps, Neighborhood Youth Corps, community action, Vista, surplus food for the needy, food stamps, and child welfare, as well as aid to the aged, blind, and disabled not covered by other social insurance programs. The $17.6 billion spent on these programs appears to be an impressive figure for a nation that is often criticized for its undernourished public sector. However, the inadequacy of this expenditure is clear: it represents 1.2 percent of our national output while a much larger portion of the population than that is living in poverty. For example, in 1968 there were 13.1 million persons, 6.5 percent of the population, under the age of 25 living in poverty. These persons could not receive old-age or retirement benefits or workman's compensation. Many have never worked because they are below 15 years of age. Children, the group with the greatest potential for improving their socioeconomic status, are the least likely to receive substantial benefits under the current structure of social welfare expenditures. If the vicious cycle of poverty is to be broken, this group of poor persons needs job training and compensatory education, as well as money to meet the immediate problems imposed by their poverty. The following section discusses national antipoverty policies. A discussion of ways to reduce the number of working people in poverty is followed by a scheme that may reduce the costs of required welfare expenditures.

NATIONAL POLICIES TO REDUCE POVERTY

A man who works full time all year and yet cannot earn enough to keep his family out of poverty suffers one of the most frustrating forms of indigence. A full-time worker who earns $1.85 per hour cannot keep an urban family of four out of poverty. Many occupations pay low wages that are the product of impersonal market forces, imposing a life of poverty on hardworking heads of households who cannot find better employment.

A frequently proposed remedy for this problem has been minimum wage legislation that guarantees every employed worker a "living wage." The classical argument against minimum wage legislation is based on the proposition that many unskilled workers are not productive enough to merit earnings higher than the market wage. In response to government action forcing an increase in the wages of unskilled workers, firms will employ fewer workers of this type. This argument is shown graphically in Figure 4.1. In the absence of government intervention, the market wage (W_m) will be at the intersection of the demand (DD) and supply (S) curves with OE_1 workers employed. A minimum wage at W will reduce the quantity of labor demanded to OE_2, while the number willing to work at that wage increases to OE_3. Under the new legislation E_3–E_2 will be unemployed. The increase in welfare experienced by the unskilled workers who remain employed is clear, although the improvement was at the expense of the workers who lost their jobs, OE_1–OE_2. Some gain but others lose, and the net gain in social welfare is uncertain.

One way to implement the minimum wage without an increase in unemployment is for the government to shift the demand for labor to $D'D'$ in Figure 4.1. In such a circumstance the government guarantees each person a job at the minimum wage ($\overline{W}$). A frequent criticism of using government as an employer of last resort is that it increases public sector employment in labor-intensive areas that are not particularly in need of expansion. To the extent the projects are of a "make work" sort, they would not increase the workers' sense of economic independ-

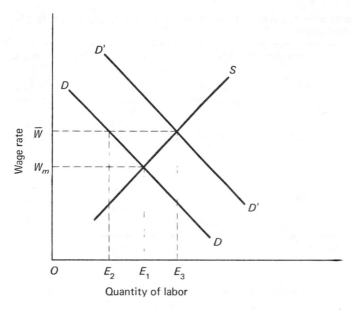

FIGURE 4.1. The effect of minimum–wage legislation on the employment of low-skilled workers.

ence. This criticism neglects the many public works that would improve the environment of our cities. Properly organized, these meaningful projects could be designed to train unskilled workers for jobs in the private sector. Such an upgrading of the labor force would, of course, require an imaginative program.

Since the Employment Act of 1946, a job for all persons seeking work has been a national goal. This legislation is in conflict with the goal of establishing a living wage for each worker. Economists have tradi- tionally argued that to increase the demand for labor, the wage rate must be lowered so that employers can afford to employ more workers. Operating as an employer of last resort, the government can eliminate the conflict between the goals of a guaranteed wage and full employ- ment. Such a policy, of course, must be supplemented by a system of transfer payments to the poor who do not participate in the labor force. The aged, the ill, and female heads of households are those in greatest need of income supplements.

The employer-of-last-resort strategy to combat poverty is based on the government's intervention in the workings of the labor market. An alternative approach to eliminate poverty is based on a program of income transfers. The concept of the negative income tax is designed to guarantee each family an income above a given standard and at the

TABLE 4.2 The impact of a hypothetical negative income tax scheme on a family of four (in dollars)

Income from all sources	Present situation		Under negative income tax	
	Income tax liability (1969)[a]	Net income	Tax payment	Net income
0	0	0	−3000	3000
1000	0	1000	−2500	3500
2000	0	2000	−2000	4000
3000	42	2958	−1500	4500
4000	170	3830	−1000	5000
5000	306	4694	−500	5500
6000	450	5550	0	6000
7000	603	6397	603[b]	6397
8000	772	7228	772[b]	7228

[a] Allows four deductions at $600 each plus a 10 percent standard deduction.
[b] Reverts back to the present mildly progressive tax structure.

same time encourage people to earn as much income as they can. A negative income tax program could be based on a poverty income for an urban family of four, e.g., $3,000. If a family earned no income, they would receive a "negative income tax" equal to the designated minimum income. Each dollar earned up to some moderate standard of living, e.g., $6,000, would reduce the negative income tax by 50 cents.[1] After reaching a moderate standard of living, the family would revert to a progressive income tax schedule that would help finance the costs of the program. Such a program is illustrated in Table 4.2.

A principal advantage of a negative income tax scheme to combat poverty is that it can replace many separate welfare programs. Moreover, because transfer payments are tied to the national income tax, recipients are less likely to feel that they are receiving charity or something similarly demeaning. A weakness lies in the potential work disincentive effects inherent in a negative income tax program. Consider, for example, a person who earns $2.00 an hour or $4,000 a year if he works full time. After the negative income tax scheme shown in Table 4.2 is instituted, he can enjoy an income of $5,000. In effect he receives $3,000 a year from the negative income tax and earns an additional $2,000. Under the new arrangement he works 2,000 hours a year for an additional $2,000. This reduction in his effective wage to $1.00 an hour may cause the worker to consume more leisure and to work less. The frequent claim that the negative income tax has no work disincentive effects is based on the assumption that workers will choose to maximize their income rather than optimize the work/leisure relationship. If workers substitute leisure for work, as economic theory suggests they will when take-home earnings are reduced, this claim is exaggerated.

If the disincentive effects of the negative income tax are substantial, such a program may not reduce poverty among the potentially productive poor and at the same time may raise welfare costs. This would frustrate the intent of the policy and hence be a major shortcoming. In such a case, the government operating as an employer of last resort would be a more effective basis for antipoverty programs. The extent of this disincentive problem is an important area for further research.

A program that raises extremely low levels of consumption may reduce the degree of myopia among youth from poor families, because more of their current consumption needs would be satisfied. It would also reduce the net financial gains realized by poor youth when they quit school, thereby reducing the opportunity cost of investing in education. Thus, such a program may have the beneficial side effect of reducing the school dropout rate. Efforts to reduce poverty must include a variety of programs to break the vicious cycle of poverty. As already noted, compensatory education for children from culturally deprived homes appears to be crucial if the cycle of poverty is to be broken.

THE URBAN UPGRADING FUNCTION

From the economic point of view, the urban upgrading function can improve the socioeconomic status only of those persons who are potentially employable. Transfer payments to alleviate poverty among unavoidably nonproductive persons can originate at any level of government. While the city may dispense these cash grants, there is little reason to believe it can accomplish this task more effectively than any other level of government. The city's role in improving the socioeconomic status of the poor is to facilitate their absorption into the mainstream of American economic life. In relatively large metropolitan areas, a wide range of employment opportunities helps persons of any skill level find employment.

A complete occupational structure, however, assures only that there is some demand for all skill levels, not that all workers of a given skill level will be able to find employment. The presence in the city of large numbers of poor persons with few skills may actually reduce the number of these people who can break the cycle of poverty. When the number of unskilled workers increases relative to the demand for their services, their wage rate is likely to fall. This increase in supply is shown by the shift of the supply curve from SS to $S'S'$ in Figure 4.2. Although

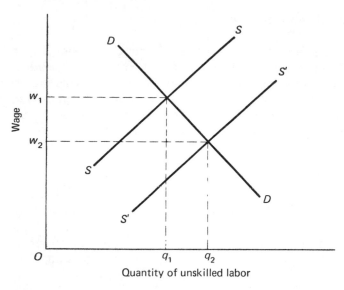

FIGURE 4.2. The impact on wages of an increase in the supply of unskilled labor.

more unskilled workers are employed (oq_1 to oq_2), their assimilation into the middle class may be retarded. The falling wage rate (w_1 to w_2) makes it more likely that the unskilled worker will find himself working full time and still unable to support his family. The resulting frustration and despair may actually reinforce the vicious cycle of poverty and the hopelessness that it implies.

The urban upgrading function will clearly work most effectively when the supply of unskilled workers is low relative to the demand for their services. When the wage rate for unskilled labor is low and insufficient to ward off poverty, the poor can do little to improve their economic position. Poor persons migrating to metropolitan areas because of declining job opportunities in rural areas are partly responsible for the large supply of unskilled workers. At the same time, the mechanization of many unskilled tasks reduces the demand for unskilled workers. Many of the potentially productive poor must compete for fewer jobs with the new arrivals who have come to the city in search of a better life. The rising supply of low-skill workers and the declining demand combine to assure that the wage rate for these occupations will not lift a family out of poverty. Because of these market constraints, the city does not have an unlimited capacity to absorb the poor into the mainstream of economic life.

The city's upgrading function is frustrated by the failure of public policy to provide job opportunities in rural areas and in small towns. Because relatively few opportunities exist in these places, most displaced workers must come to cities in search of employment. Their inability to earn a decent living, due to the enlarged supply of low-skilled workers, creates a sense of failure and frustration. As a result, the number of workers and their children who are upgraded may be smaller than it would be if the market wage for unskilled labor were higher and fewer were employed.

Policies of the national government can facilitate the urban upgrading function in two ways. First, reducing migration to the city, by offering or encouraging the creation of employment opportunities in rural areas, would give unskilled workers in the city a better chance to break the cycle of poverty. Their upgrading would in time reduce the supply of unskilled workers, thereby improving the outlook for others seeking to improve their economc status. Second, as already noted, if the federal government maintained a reasonable minimum wage as an employer of last resort, the poor would be less subject to the market forces that frustrate the city's upgrading function.

Low wages are not the only barrier inhibiting the upward mobility of the potentially productive poor. A large portion of the poor reside in the central city and are somewhat isolated from the increasing number of job opportunities in the outlying suburban areas. In 1970 over 62 percent of the poor in metropolitan areas lived in the central city. At the same time almost one-half of all manufacturing jobs, the major source of high-wage occupations, were located in the suburban ring.

The relatively large distance between the residences of the poor and job sites is likely to reduce their economic well-being.[2] Public transportation from the central city to suburban job sites often does not exist. In such cases, central city residents without sufficient income to purchase an automobile cannot reach potential places of employment. When public transportation is available, it is often costly in terms of both time and money. This lowers the effective hourly wage-rate received by the worker. Given preferences between work and leisure, these costs lower the price of leisure and will tend to increase the amount of leisure consumed. This tendency may be offset in part by the response to lower income, i.e., the decline in income may increase work effort. The relative strengths of the above income gain and leisure substitution effects determine the net impact of segregation on work effort.

Perhaps more important is the fact that segregation of the poor reduces the amount of information about jobs available to them. One study indicates that about one-third of all jobs are acquired via information obtained from friends or relatives.[3] Less than 20 percent are obtained from "formal" methods of job search such as public and private employment agencies, want ads, and unions. When a group is segregated and is generally underemployed, its members do not have access to a major mechanism for getting desirable employment: referral by friends and relatives.

A large number of poor people in a city does not necessarily imply a breakdown in the urban upgrading function. Successful operation of the upgrading function is indicated by *how long* potentially productive people *stay* poor in the city. If generation after generation remain poor, the upgrading function is clearly being frustrated. The city has traditionally upgraded minority groups. Foreign immigrants, the Irish, Germans, Poles, Italians, and others, accounted for a large portion of the urban poor for many decades. These groups have by and large been integrated into the mainstream of American economic life. Blacks are the largest single group of poor persons in many cities today. It is harder for blacks to become integrated into the economic mainstream than it was for foreign immigrants, for two reasons. First, the educational attainment required for most jobs is rising, making it difficult for unskilled workers in the modern city to find suitable employment. By contrast, foreign immigrant groups entered an economy in which low-skilled occupations and low educational attainment were the rule rather than the exception. Secondly, nonwhite minorities in the modern city may face greater discrimination than that experienced by their foreign-born predecessors. The special case of the black poor is discussed in the following section.

POVERTY: THE SPECIAL CASE OF BLACKS

Poverty affects black families more often than whites. Over 24 percent of all blacks living in metropolitan areas received an income below subsistence in 1970. In contrast, the incidence of poverty among whites was 7.3 percent. The poverty problem of blacks is in many ways similar to that of other groups. Low productivity is a major reason for their low income; increasing the educational achievement of blacks is the principal vehicle for increasing their effectiveness as members of the labor force. As already noted, the maintenance of tight labor markets is a necessary precondition for the economic advance of the black as well as white poor.

The economic plight of the black poor is complicated by discrimination that reduces both job and housing opportunities. Effective discrimination, however, does more than just reduce the actual number of economic opportunities. By reducing the expected payoff from increasing educational achievement, discrimination helps to perpetuate the impoverished status quo. The failure syndrome, which can be a major barrier to the economic advance of the poor, is likely to be particularly strong among minorities that suffer discrimination.

While discrimination is an important determinant of the incomes of blacks, empirical estimates of its impact are generally speculative. The simplest way to quantify the effect of discrimination is to assume that it causes all differences between black and white incomes. This approach may not be altogether inappropriate, since these income differences could be the result of the indirect as well as direct discrimination that has occurred over the past 300 years. Assuming that innate ability does not vary by race, this estimation procedure reflects the total impact of discrimination. A principal weakness of this approach is that it combines past and present discrimination. Since historical discrimination must be taken as a given, a more useful estimate of inequality of opportunity should focus on present discrimination, which may be susceptible to correction through public policy.

Discrimination plays an important role in complicating the process of economic advance among blacks. Estimating the impact of discrimination, of course, is difficult. Several studies suggest that discrimination reduces the income of blacks by at least 15 percent.[4] These estimates take the educational level of blacks as given, i.e., assume that it is not affected by discrimination. Since both the quantity and quality of education achieved by blacks may be affected by discrimination, this estimate may be too low.

Discrimination also reduces the amount of housing available to blacks. Dwellings otherwise open to the poor are frequently closed to minority groups. As a result of this discrimination, the black poor are more concentrated in the central city than are their white counterparts. In 1970 almost 80 percent of the black poor in metropolitan areas were residents of the central city, while only 55 percent of the white poor shared this isolation from suburban jobs. To the extent that segregation of the poor in the central city reduces employment opportunities, discrimination in housing places an additional burden on the black poor hoping to improve their economic status.

Public policy can be utilized in various ways to reduce discrimination. One such method, moral suasion, consists of public statements by the government encouraging a suspension of discriminatory behavior. This hortatory approach is popular because it is not expensive to implement and forces no change of behavior in the offender. Although moral suasion may be employed frequently, it will probably be ineffective because of its toothless nature. A related strategy is to pass legislation that prohibits discriminatory behavior and establishes penalties for violators. Legislation passed in the post–World War II period has attempted to eliminate job discrimination, integrate schools and housing, and guarantee minority voting rights. While considerable resources may be required to enforce such legislation, the mere threat of legal action may succeed in reducing the propensity to discriminate against minority groups.

Another, more potent, way in which public policy can be used to upgrade minority groups lies in government itself being an equal opportunity employer. The total impact of such a policy depends, of course, on the labor skills demanded by government. Workers in the public sector generally have more schooling than those employed by private business enterprises. Only 23 percent of the workers employed by government in 1960 had no high school training, compared to 38 percent of those in the private sector. Thus the effect of equal opportunity employment policies on the economic well-being of the black poor is likely to be minor because of their relatively low level of education. Of course, if the skills acceptable to the public sector changed because government became an employer of last resort or engaged in on-the-job training, this policy could have a major impact on the economic well-being of the black poor.

The government, particularly at the federal level, has yet another role to play in raising the income of blacks. Through the use of its formidable contractual power, the federal government may force a significant proportion of the private sector to have equal opportunity employment practices. The strength of federal contracts as a policy tool to move blacks up the job ladder has been documented by Herbert R. Northrup.[5] He argues that the aerospace industry has been a more than fair employer of blacks to the point of discrimination against whites because the government desired more blacks on the payroll even when layoffs were in progress. The success of this program in the aerospace industry has not been realized in other industries. A more recent and systematic analysis of black occupational standing found that industries involved in federal government contracting hire fewer rather than more blacks relative to whites.[6]

Frustration over ineffective government programs to help the black poor has led many ghetto residents to consider self-help programs designed to increase the level of economic activity in the ghetto. A simple analytical device can be used to investigate many of these self-help proposals. Aggregate income (Y) for a group of persons, e.g., residents of a ghetto, is equal to income earned by resident labor outside the ghetto (E) plus consumption expenditures within the ghetto (C). In other words, a ghetto resident may earn income by working for a firm outside the ghetto (E) or by providing goods or services to other ghetto residents (C). For simplicity, ghetto consumption is assumed to be some linear function of income. We have:

(1) $Y = C + E$

(2) $C = a + bY$

where b is the proportion of an additional dollar of income that would be spent in the ghetto. By substitution and rearrangement:

(3) $Y = (a + E)/1 - b.$

The term $1/1 - b$ is called the multiplier and determines the total increase in income as a result of increased earnings from outside the ghetto. For example, assume the typical ghetto resident spends one-half of an additional dollar of earnings in the ghetto ($b = .5$). A one-dollar increase in earnings from outside the ghetto will yield a two-dollar increase in total ghetto income ($\Delta E/1 - b$). Equation (3) shows there are two basic determinants of aggregate ghetto income: export earnings (E) and the marginal propensity to consume ghetto-produced goods and services (b). This framework is useful to evaluate various self-help schemes that have been devised by minority groups.

Increasing the opportunity of blacks to own small business is one popular approach, called "black capitalism," to increasing the income of this minority group. It is asumed that these minority-run enterprises will increase black earnings by employing blacks and also provide increased opportunities to purchase black-produced goods and services. Further, it is hoped that these black entrepreneurs will head growing businesses that provide an ever increasing number of jobs for black workers. Thus the purpose of black capitalism is to increase earnings from nonminority sources (ΔE) and at the same time increase the propensity of blacks to buy products produced by minority enterprises (b).

The increase in earnings that may accrue to blacks from the expansion of small businesses is likely to be modest. All new small business firms are very apt to fail—fewer than one-half survive two years. Survival of black-owned firms in the ghetto is further threatened by high insurance rates and the low level of personal income in the area. Because of the large economies of scale in many manufacturing industries, small businesses tend to begin in service activities, where entry is easy and exit frequent. In 1964, for example, over 45 percent of all black enterprises in Philadelphia ghettos were engaged in hairdressing, barbering, or food services. Luncheonettes, the *most* prosperous of these firms, had a median annual sales of $6,800.[7] A survey conducted by the National Business League revealed that the average black business sold $19,147 worth of goods or services in 1968. Neither was the growth of employment opportunities for blacks impressive: The average firm hired 2.2 full-time employees and 1.1 part-time workers.[8] This poor performance is not surprising in light of the low income of most blacks. Also, if whites prefer to purchase services from white-owned businesses, black entrepreneurs are virtually without a market for their output. The meager sales and low employment of these businesses suggest that the change in earnings (ΔE) resulting from attempts to foster black capitalism are likely to be modest. Although the lack of business skills may hinder these entrepreneurs, the dominance of large corporations in most industries may be the largest barrier to the effective use of small minority-owned enterprises as a method to raise black incomes.

The performance of black-owned enterprises also suggests they do not raise the level of black income by increasing the multiplier ($1/(1 - b)$). The entrepreneur, if he personally profits from the business, will probably not spend his money in ghetto luncheonettes and hairdressing establishments. More likely he will purchase consumer durables, cars and other items that are commonly consumed by the white middle class and that are produced by corporations in the white community. Any success that a black entrepreneur enjoys does not tend to stimulate community development, in part because the concept of black capitalism is based on an individualistic ethic, not one of cooperative improvement for many people.

Black capitalism is an approach to ghetto development based on the traditional American attitude toward entrepreneurship. It often relies on the myth of Horatio Alger, suggesting that with initiative and a little equity capital, there is no limit to personal advance. Unfortunately, the common plight of small businessmen who possess some capital and much initiative, whether black or white, reveals the false promise of black capitalism. An approach with much more potential is that of the community development corporation (CDC). The CDC is typically a nonprofit organization formed to enhance the economic power of a particular poor community. As a catalyst for community development, CDCs are more effective than are black capitalists because of their potential to attract support from outside the ghetto. "Because CDCs are broad based, have social objectives and are not organizations of a small number of businessmen who stand to make private profits, they become a politically 'legitimate' vehicle through which foundations, government agencies and private donors can make contributions—usually tax exempt—of equity capital."[9]

Although superior to black capitalism, the impact of the community development corporation on employment opportunities in the black ghetto is likely to be modest. Ultimately all attempts to increase employment opportunities in poor communities through local ownership must face the reality that most stable, high-wage activities in America are dominated by large corporations. While the CDC can play an important role in encouraging the development of human and physical resources of the community, it must be part of a more ambitious antipoverty program.

Ghetto-initiated programs to improve the economic status of blacks are unlikely to have a major impact on their level of income. Given the inability of the public sector to deal effectively with discrimination, it appears that the interests of urban minorities might best be served if the nation adopted a comprehensive effort to eliminate poverty. The basic elements of such an effort, as outlined in Chapter 3, are transfer payments to persons unable to work, special education for children from culturally deprived backgrounds, and the maintenance of tight labor markets with government operating as an employer of last resort.

NOTES

[1] In general, the income bracket that has a zero tax rate is determined by the minimum income divided by the tax rate. If the negative income tax is reduced by 25 rather than 50 cents for each dollar earned, the break-even income would rise to $12,000.

[2] See J. D. Mooney, "Housing Segregation, Negro Employment and Metropolitan Decentralization," *The Quarterly Journal of Economics* 83 (May 1969): 299–311.

[3] E. Rayack and M. Lurie, "Racial Differences in Migration and Job Search," *Southern Economic Journal* 33 (July 1966): 81–95.

[4] See Gary S. Becker, *The Economics of Discrimination* (University of Chicago Press, 1957), ch. 2; James D. Gwartney, "Discrimination and Income Differentials," *American Economic Review* 60 (June 1970): 396–408; and D. W. Rasmussen, "Discrimination and the Income of Non-White Men," *American Journal of Economics and Sociology, 30* (October 1971): 377–382.

[5] H. R. Northrup, "In-Plant Movement of Negroes in the Aerospace Industry," *Monthly Labor Review* 91 (February 1968): 22–25.

[6] Barbara R. Bergman and Jerolyn R. Lyle, "The Occupational Standing of Negroes by Areas and Industries," *Journal of Human Resources* 6 (Fall 1971): 411–433.

[7] Eugene P. Foley, "The Negro Businessmen: In Search of a Tradition," in Talcott Parsons and Kenneth B. Clark, *The Negro American* (Boston: Beacon Press, 1967), p. 561.

[8] Geoffrey Faux, "Background Paper," in *CDCs: New Hope for the Inner City* (New York: Twentieth Century Fund, 1971), p. 45.

[9] Ibid., p. 54.

RECOMMENDED READING

Mooney, Joseph D. "Housing Segregation, Negro Employment and Metropolitan Decentralization," *The Quarterly Journal of Economics* 83 (May 1969): 299–311.

Rasmussen, David W. "Discrimination and the Income of Non-White Men," *American Journal of Economics and Sociology,* 30 (October 1971): 377–382.

Schoor, Alvin. "Against a Negative Income Tax," *The Public Interest* 5 (Fall 1966): 110–116.

Tabb, William K. *The Political Economy of the Black Ghetto.* New York: Norton, 1970.

Task Force on Community Development Corporations. *CDCs: New Hope for the Inner City.* New York: Twentieth Century Fund, 1971.

Tobin, James. "The Case for an Income Guarantee," *The Public Interest,* Summer 1966, pp. 31–41.

U.S. Department of Labor. "The Irregular Economy and the AFDC Mother," *Manpower Report of the President—1968,* Washington, D.C., 1968. Reprinted in D. W. Rasmussen and C. T. Haworth, eds., *The Modern City: A Book of Readings.* New York: Harper & Row, 1973.

5
THE LOCATION OF ECONOMIC ACTIVITY AND THE SURVIVAL OF THE CENTRAL CITY

A metropolitan area provides the spatial organization for the business firms and residents that account for the region's economic activity. Urban physical form to some extent determines the effectiveness of the city, that is, its ability to provide externalities in production, economies of scale in consumption, and the upgrading function. These considerations suggest three basic issues in urban economics that are related to the location of economic activity. The first is the decline and decay of the central city portion of many major metropolitan areas. At stake is the question of whether or not the traditional high-density central city and its nucleus, the central business district (CBD) can remain a viable spatial arrangement for economic and residential activity. Secondly, some arrangements of residences and employment opportunities may be more effective than others in upgrading members of the lower socio-economic strata. Finally, because the city and its functions are based on the interdependence of the economic units operating within its borders, it often fosters unintended third-party effects or negative externalities. Keeping these adverse side effects in check is in large measure a problem of spatial organization.

The survival of the central city

Discussions of the viability of the central city and its central business district often fail to focus on the purposes of the city and therefore do not place the policy alternatives in proper perspective. William Alonso has argued:

Without positive action the urban center may wither, and the metropolis may become a vast, amorphous, headless amoeba. A strong center is needed socially, economically and psychologically, for it is here that urban life is lived in full, and virtually all activities in the metropolitan area focus towards it. . . . The downtown area is the brain tissue of the metropolis, a complex, evolving, and little-understood organ. If it is sick, it may require surgery, but this surgery should be done with sensitive fingers, with the finest surgical instruments, and with the closest attention to what in fact is being done.[1]

A less reverent view of the traditional center of economic activity is offered by a noted political scientist:

. . . the core city is treated as a heart of a metropolitan area that may become diseased and thus suffer dire ill not only to itself but extending to the whole metropolitan body. No vital statistics on central city heart attacks are offered, however, nor any evidence on metropolitan bodies suffering from central city heart disease. The metaphor sometimes presents itself as the central city in the role of a tree and the suburbs as clinging parasitic vines who are destined to fall with the tree in a common fate. Again the metaphor is not designed to lead to factual translation but to poetic and evocative conviction. The rhetoric of political persuasion and nostalgic sentimental mysticism is designed to avoid both facts and rational analysis.[2]

It is undeniable that high-density central cities have declined in the past two decades. Table 5.1 shows the population trends in the 18 older metropolitan areas that had a central city with a population exceeding 250,000 in 1910. The population residing in the central city portion of these metropolitan areas fell from 27.2 million to 25.9 million in the two decades following 1950. Only three of these central cities increased in population, the major exception being Los Angeles, which gained over 900,000 people. If Los Angeles is excluded from the sample, the modest 4 percent decline in central city population increases to 8 percent.

These older cities, largely built before the widespread use of the private automobile, have a high population density. Urban populations were highly concentrated in the preautomobile era because of the problems of intraurban transportation. The median population density per square mile for these 18 central cities is 11,061, the least dense being New Orleans (2,858), while New York (25,996) has the most concentrated population. The core cities that can most easily facilitate the use of the private automobile appear to be the least susceptible to decline. The three older cities (Los Angeles, Milwaukee, and New Orleans) that experienced an increase in population from 1950 to 1970 were the least densely populated, averaging 5,662 persons per square mile.

Population trends in the young major metropolitan areas are consistent with the notion that growth occurs in those places that adapt to the private automobile. Younger central cities, those reaching a popula-

TABLE 5.1 Population trends in old major metropolitan areas, 1950–1970ᵃ (in thousands)

SMSA	SMSA population		Central city population			
	1950	1970	1950	1970	Change	1970 density/sq. mi.
Baltimore	1,337.4	2,045.2	949.7	895.2	−54.5	11,477
Boston	2,370.0	2,730.2	801.4	628.2	−173.2	13,657
Buffalo	1,089.2	1,334.5	580.1	457.8	−122.3	11,166
Chicago	5,495.4	6,892.5	3,621.0	3,322.9	−298.1	14,968
Cleveland	1,465.5	2,043.4	914.8	739.0	−175.8	9,723
Detroit	3,016.2	4,163.5	1,849.0	1,492.9	−356.7	10,818
Jersey City	NA	597.1	299.0	253.5	−45.5	16,898
Los Angeles	4,367.9	6,974.1	2,221.1	3,128.8	907.7	6,245
Milwaukee	871.0	1,393.3	637.4	709.5	72.1	7,884
Minneapolis	1,116.5	1,805.1	833.1	740.7	−92.4	7,054
New Orleans	685.4	1,034.3	570.4	585.8	15.4	2,858
New York	NA	11,448.0	7,892.0	7,798.8	−93.2	25,996
Newark	NA	1,847.5	438.8	378.2	−60.6	15,759
Philadelphia	3,671.0	4,777.4	2,071.6	1,927.9	−143.7	14,945
Pittsburgh	2,213.0	2,383.8	676.8	512.8	−164.0	9,323
St. Louis	1,681.3	2,331.0	856.8	607.7	−249.1	9,962
San Francisco	2,240.8	3,069.8	1,159.9	1,062.7	−97.2	10,956
Washington, D.C.	1,464.1	2,835.7	802.2	746.2	−56.0	12,232

ᵃOld major SMSAs had a central city with a population greater than 250,000 in 1910.
SOURCES: U.S. Bureau of the Census, *1970 Census of Population, Preliminary Reports* (PC [p3]–3, November 1970); *Statistical Abstract of the United States, 1966* and *1970* (Washington, D.C.: Government Printing Office, 1966 and 1970).

tion of 250,000 after 1910, did not experience a decline in population. As Table 5.2 shows, 21 of 27 of these cities increased their population over this two-decade span, accounting for a net increase in central city residents of 59 percent, or 4.7 million. The median population density per square mile for these cities is 5,653, a figure about one-half the density of the older central cities.[3]

In both young and old major metropolitan areas, the central city population has declined relative to the suburban ring. Central city residents as a proportion of metropolitan population fell from .68 in 1950 to a 1970 figure of .44 in older metropolitan areas. The same ratio fell from .59 to .48 in younger SMSAs. Some analysts observe this decline and conclude that the urban core is deteriorating. In a growing metropolitan area with fixed central city boundaries, this relative decline is inevitable. Since absolute decline is the clearest indication of central city decay, this problem is most prevalent in older metropolitan areas where high population densities characterize the urban core.

Rescuing the traditional high-density central city from a process of continuous decline is a major policy question when considering the

TABLE 5.2 Population trends in young major metropolitan areas, 1950–1970[a] (in thousands)

SMSA	SMSA population		Central city population			
	1950	1970	1950	1970	Change	1970 density per sq. mi.
Akron	410.0	673.5	274.6	273.3	−1.3	5,156
Atlanta	671.8	1,373.6	331.3	487.6	156.2	3,585
Austin	160.9	295.5	132.5	251.8	119.3	5,595
Birmingham	558.9	730.0	326.0	297.4	−28.6	4,720
Cincinnati	904.4	1,373.2	504.0	448.5	−55.5	5,825
Columbus	503.4	904.7	375.9	533.4	157.5	6,131
Dallas	614.8	1,539.4	434.5	836.1	401.6	3,292
Dayton	457.3	842.2	243.9	239.6	−4.3	7,046
Denver	563.8	1,223.1	415.8	512.7	96.9	7,539
Fort Worth	361.3	757.1	278.8	388.1	109.3	2,812
Houston	806.7	1,958.5	596.2	1,213.1	616.9	3,779
Indianapolis	552.0	1,099.6	427.2	742.6	315.4	10,609
Kansas City	814.4	1,240.6	456.6	495.4	38.8	3,811
Louisville	576.9	819.1	369.1	356.9	−12.2	6,050
Memphis	482.4	767.0	396.0	620.9	224.9	4,813
Miami	495.1	1,259.2	249.3	331.6	82.3	9,752
Phoenix	331.8	963.1	106.8	580.3	473.5	3,103
Portland	704.8	992.6	373.6	375.2	1.6	5,684
Rochester	487.6	875.6	332.5	293.7	−38.8	7,938
Sacramento	359.5	800.6	137.6	254.4	116.8	5,653
San Diego	556.8	1,318.0	334.4	675.8	341.4	3,466
San Jose	290.6	1,064.7	95.2	443.9	348.7	7,926
Seattle	733.0	1,404.4	467.6	487.5	19.9	5,945
Tampa	409.1	999.6	221.4	487.5	266.1	3,996
Toledo	395.6	685.5	303.6	379.1	75.5	7,737
Tulsa	251.7	471.7	182.7	327.9	145.2	6,693
Wichita	223.3	386.0	168.3	274.4	106.1	5,381

[a] Young major metropolitan areas had a central city population exceeding 250,000 in 1970, but reached this figure after 1910.
SOURCES: U.S. Bureau of the Census, *1970 Census of Population,* Preliminary Reports (PC [p3]–3, November 1970); *Statistical Abstract of the United States, 1966* and *1970* (Washington, D.C.: Government Printing Office, 1966 and 1970).

location of economic activity. The advantages of urban agglomeration outlined in Chapter 2 suggest the issues underlying the emotionally charged debates on the survival of the central city. One purpose of the city is to foster economies of scale in consumption. The existence of a high-density central city in a metropolitan area increases consumer choice in two ways. Certain types of retail and service activity can be provided only in areas of high population density.

. . . this variety and richness is possible only because there are enough things and enough people downtown to attract more things and more people. Let the size of the downtown area drop below the necessary critical mass, and dissolution will follow. There will not be enough six-foot girls coming downtown for there to be a shop especially for them. There will not be enough lunch time demand to keep fine restaurants going, and if there are no restaurants, the theaters will suffer. Unless downtown is big enough, there will be no downtown. Some activities will move to the suburbs, but many will die or will never come into existence. Life will become much duller and more homogenized.[4]

A traditional central city also offers consumers an option for high-density living. Aggregate consumer welfare may be greatly improved if a high-quality environment is offered at various levels of population density. Population density can affect the way of life of people; the differences in style are easily illustrated. When desiring to purchase a commodity in the late evening, residents of low-density suburbs must drive to a late night store, whereas those in the traditional central city may walk if they wish.[5] There is no reason to assume one life style is "better" than the other, and the city provides an economy of scale in consumption by offering residents a choice. Cities in modern America are better than they were at the turn of the century from the viewpoint of consumer choice. In 1900 virtually all residents had to reside in high-density areas while only the very wealthy could afford the luxury of a home outside the city. Many modern cities offer consumers a choice between high- and low-density living. Maintaining the high-density alternative is a key issue of urban policy. A major portion of this chapter is devoted to the analysis of the viability of maintaining areas of high density in our major metropolitan areas.

The upgrading function

Residential segregation and its effect on the upward mobility of minority groups is a second issue related to the use of urban land. Reasons for the income segregation that characterizes most of our major metropolitan areas are analyzed in the discussion of residential location presented in this chapter. The impact of this physical isolation of the poor on the city's ability to absorb them into the mainstream of American economic life was analyzed in the preceding chapter.

The elimination of negative externalities

Interdependence of all economic activity is a principal characteristic of urban life. The negative externalities, or adverse third-party effects, resulting from this mutual interdependence are often a product of inappropriate land-use patterns. Noise generated by an airport, for example, will lower the welfare of many households in adjacent residential areas. Because they affect the environment adversely, many industrial activities should not be located near large residential populations. Methods of reducing negative externalities that are a product of the spatial arrangement of economic activity are discussed in this chapter.

A THEORETICAL FOUNDATION: THE RENT GRADIENT

Because all residential and commercial activities require land, the cost of space plays an important role in determining their location. As the amount of land relative to other factors required by an economic activity increases, the importance of land costs in location decisions rises. Patterns of land use in metropolitan areas will thus be shaped by the spatial distribution of land costs. Of course, land costs are in turn affected by patterns of land use.

Some locations in the city command a relatively high price because many land users find the site attractive. Aggregations of economic activity, such as the central business district of older metropolitan areas, rest on high-priced land because of the high demand for a limited amount of space. Despite the availability of cheap land on the urban fringe, the difficulty of moving people within the city and problems of intercity transportation made a central city location particularly desirable in the preautomobile era.[6] The use of the railroad for intercity transportation made it advantageous for most firms to locate near the terminal that was typically close to the central business district. Transportation, communications, and production technologies were responsible for a land-use pattern that was dominated by the central business district.

A simple model can explain the pattern of land costs common to many of this country's urban areas. All economic activity is assumed to take place in a relatively small geographic area such as the CBD. For urban areas during the preautomobile industrial era, this assumption is not a serious violation of reality. If a fixed portion of a family's budget is to be spent on location, it must be divided between transportation and rent. The location or land rent of a site is therefore a payment to the owner for time and transportation costs that are saved by living there.[7] *Land rent* in economics is not to be confused with the term *rent* as applied in everyday language. Land rent is a payment for an advantage one piece of real estate has over another because of its location. A landowner receives income from his property because it provides a service to the user. If his property is at an advantageous location or is in some other way unique, he may receive an additional payment called land rent. Land rent is typically highest in the CBD because there are virtually no transportation costs associated with travel between the place of residence and other economic activities. At a considerable distance from the urban center, property sites will receive no land rent because of the high costs of transportation to the central business districts. In general, land rents are highest at the center of economic activity and decline to zero at the urban fringe. This relationship between land rent and distance from the central business district is called the *rent gradient*.

The market price of land is determined by the net present value of earnings the owner can expect to receive in the future. As already noted, the owner will receive income for the services that the land provides and may receive land rents if the real estate is at an advantageous location. Since property located near the CBD offers savings in both time and transportation costs, rents can be charged; the price of land is thus higher in that part of the metropolitan area.[8]

Although the above model is based on a degree of central city dominance that no longer exists, it nevertheless offers insight into the location of economic activity. There are two important sources that account for the model's continued relevance. Most important is the fact that empirical estimates of the relationship between land rent and distance from the central business district show the expected decline in rents toward the urban fringe.[9] Secondly, the model could easily be adapted to the multicentered urban area that may typify the future. The rent gradient can shed light on the decline of the central city and the expansion of economic activity in the suburban portion of many urban areas. In the following section, changes in the location of manufacturing activity are shown to be a product of the interaction of transportation and production technologies with the rent gradient.

THE LOCATION OF MANUFACTURING

Since World War II, changes in manufacturing activity in central cities are similar to those of population. Table 5.3 shows that manufacturing employment increased from 4.25 million to 4.39 million in the central cities of major metropolitan areas between 1947 and 1967. Older metropolitan areas suffered a 7.7 percent decline in manufacturing employment, which was more than offset by the increase of such employment in younger cities. These data confirm that central city decline is primarily a problem in the older metropolitan areas, which are characterized by relatively high population densities.

The location of manufacturing activity within a metropolitan area is

TABLE 5.3 Change in central city manufacturing employment by age of major metropolitan area, 1947–1967 (in thousands)

	1947	1967	Change	Percentage change
Old SMSAs[a]	3270.0	3016.9	−253.1	−7.7
Young SMSAs[b]	980.1	1372.3	392.2	40.0
Total	4250.1	4389.2	139.1	3.3

[a] Old SMSAs had a central city with a population greater than 250,000 in 1910.
[b] Young SMSAs are those with a central city that reached 250,000 after 1910. These are listed in Tables 5.1 and 5.2.
SOURCE: U.S. Bureau of the Census, *1967 Census of Manufactures,* vols. II and III (Washington, D.C.: Government Printing Office, 1967).

determined by the interaction of the demand for output and costs of production as they vary with distance from the central business district. Most older models of industrial location assume that the demand for output falls as the firm moves further from the bulk of the population, which is clustered around the central business district. This outdated approach suggests that it is to the financial advantage of all firms to locate close to the urban center.

In the late nineteenth and early twentieth centuries, production costs were lowest in the CBD because of the high costs of moving people over long distances within a city and the dependence on rail facilities for intercity transportation. Whether a firm sold its output locally or "exported" it to other metropolitan areas, transportation costs were minimized by a central city location. Transportation technology during the preautomobile era made it profitable for all urban economic activity to be concentrated near the central business district. The individualized transportation made possible by the automobile and truck greatly reduced the cost advantages associated with central city locations. Production technologies that were more land-intensive became profitable as the more flexible transportation system developed. In particular, the linear production assembly line required much more land than the multistory lofts used by manufacturers in central city locations. The lower-cost suburban plants could use truck transportation within the metropolitan area and among regions. Industries that sell most of their output outside the metropolitan area, known in regional economics as the "export base," face a demand for their product that is essentially unaffected by their location within the city.[10]

The relationship between land costs and the location of manufacturing activity can be presented graphically. Land requirements in the production process suggest that the cost of output will vary with distance from the central business district. Variations in cost due to location for export base activities in the preautomobile era are shown by the average cost curve *Ceb'* in Figure 5.1. Reliance on rail transportation caused costs to rise rapidly at greater distances from the CBD. Demand for the output of basic industries is essentially independent of location and is represented by the horizontal line *Deb* in the same figure.[11] The vertical distance between the demand and cost curve reflects the relative advantage of various locations to the business firm. During the preautomobile era, all the locations beyond distance *OA* from the central business district were unprofitable.

Any factor that raises the price of land near the urban center (*O*) or lowers the costs of production in outlying locations will cause firms to move further from the central business district. The widespread use of automobile and truck transportation has been a dominant force in the reduction of costs in outlying areas. As a result of this development, it became possible to take advantage of the reduced land costs on the fringe of the metropolitan area. Consequently, production costs at a distance from the CBD were reduced, the size of the savings depending on the importance of land costs in the productive process. At extreme distances from the CBD, costs rise because of the increased transportation costs for factors of production. Firms located on the fringe of the metropolitan area may not enjoy as many agglomeration economies as firms nearer to the urban core. The cost function common to export base activities in the modern automobile era is shown by curve *Ceb* in Figure 5.1. Locations near the CBD that were previously profitable are

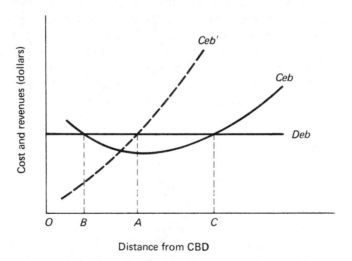

FIGURE 5.1. The impact of land costs on the location of manufactures.

now unprofitable. Locations that are feasible in the long run for most manufacturing firms are between distances *OA* and *OB*.

Unlike most activities that make up a region's economic base, a few manufacturing industries may be so dependent on agglomeration economies that their optimum location remains in the central business district. Edgar Hoover and Raymond Vernon have labeled these industries "communication oriented." Their description suggests that industries provide a shaky foundation for the continued existence of the CBD.

> A clue to the reasons for the heavy clustering of these industries is to be found in the interrelations of speed, small size and uncertainty of outlook. . . . Time is of the essence in the output of these industries, and its essentiality introduces a new dimension in the nature of the product or service being offered. Consider the printer of legal briefs or financial prospectuses; his production cycle—the lapse of time between the moment when he receives the manuscript and the time he delivers the finished product—is critical to his existence.
>   . . . the specifications of these products cannot ordinarily be anticipated; they are "unstandardized" products for the most part, often created by a process of consultation between consumer and manufacturer.[12]

These communication-oriented industries do little to enhance the viability of the central city as a location for manufacturing activity. In their study of New York, Hoover and Vernon identified about 30 industries as communication oriented. These industries accounted for less than 7 percent of all manufacturing employment in 1967. Furthermore, modern developments in telecommunications reduce the need for face-to-face meetings of business executives, while air travel makes intercity trips relatively quick and inexpensive. In a modern society such as ours, communications are sufficiently advanced that few industries are required by their quest for profits to locate in a high-density central city. Many of the so-called communication-oriented industries may have technologies that do not require much land and thus have little incentive to move from their traditional location in the urban core. The fact that Los Angeles, the nation's second largest metropolitan area, does not have a high-density urban core suggests that the importance of communication-oriented industries is likely to be exaggerated.

TRENDS IN THE LOCATION OF NONMANUFACTURING EMPLOYMENT

High-density central cities have also declined in importance as a location for nonmanufacturing activity. In the case of retail and wholesale trade, traditional urban centers suffered an absolute decline in employ-ment, in addition to the decline they experienced relative to the subur-ban ring. As shown in Table 5.4, employment in selected services in-creased 59 percent in older central cities between 1947 and 1967. This increase of 389,600 service jobs offset the decline in wholesale and retail trade and is responsible for the modest 2 percent increase in nonmanufacturing employment in older central cities. As in the case of manufacturing, the newer metropolitan areas increased their em-ployment in each of the three nonmanufacturing activities. The in-crease of 460,700 jobs in these activities represents a 40 percent increase in employment from 1947 to 1967 in these cities.

Decline of the aging central city as a center for retailing consumer goods is not surprising in light of the exodus of population from that part of older metropolitan areas. The location of retailing activity is determined by the distribution of consumers in the region. A consumer tends to shop at stores located near his home unless a more distant store is for some reason more attractive.[13] As the population has spilled into the urban fringe areas, the suburbanization of retail activity is a logical outcome.

Wholesalers are subject to less intense pressure to respond to changes in the location of the population because they sell to retailers rather than the final consumer. Since these retailers are located all around the metropolitan area, a central location may offer the whole-

TABLE 5.4 Changes in central city nonmanufacturing employment by age of major metropolitan area, 1947–1967 (in thousands)

Employment	1947	1967	Change	Percentage change
Retailing				
Old SMSAs	1737.4	1497.1	−240.3	−14
Young SMSAs	633.3	750.2	116.9	18
Wholesaling				
Old SMSAs	963.3	893.7	−69.6	−7
Young SMSAs	295.0	437.0	142.0	48
Selected Services				
Old SMSAs	662.0	1051.6	389.6	59
Young SMSAs	212.1	413.9	201.8	95
Total				
Old SMSAs	3362.7	3442.4	79.7	2
Young SMSAs	1140.4	1601.1	460.7	40

SOURCES: U.S. Bureau of the Census, *1948 Census of Business,* vols. III, V, and VII; *1967 Census of Business,* vols. II and V (Washington, D.C.: Government Printing Office, 1948 and 1967). For definitions of old and new SMSAs, see notes, Table 5.3.

saler somewhat lower transportation costs than would sites on the urban fringe. The small decline in wholesaling employment relative to retailing in the central city portion of older metropolitan areas reflects this independence of location.

Service jobs are the one exception to the general employment decline in older central cities, in part because no technological developments have reduced the cost of production at suburban sites relative to the urban core. Personal and business services account for about two-thirds of the employment in selected services. Business services, like wholesale trade, may continue to find a central city site acceptable because it is relatively accessible to client firms wherever they are located. One might expect a reduction in personal service activities in the older central cities since these businesses might follow the population to the suburbs. The large number of small firms in most of these services suggests easy entry into these activities. As noted in the previous chapter, a great portion of the economic activity in the poverty-stricken areas of our older cities is in personal services, such as barbering and hairdressing. The increase in service employment in older central cities exaggerates the number of new jobs because many poor persons are underemployed in these occupations.

White-collar employment in other services and professional fields has increased in high-density central cities. Data are available for seven older central cities whose boundaries coincide with those of the county.[14] In these cities employment in the fields of finance, insurance, real estate, medicine, law, education, and nonprofit organizations rose from 292,363 in 1948 to almost 1.2 million in 1967. Although most of this increase occurred in New York City, employment in these white-collar activities rose 150 percent in the six smaller cities. These white-collar occupations are growing faster than other sectors of the economy and may be a major source of central city employment in the future.

THE LOCATION OF RESIDENCES

Suburban America has grown rapidly in the post–World War II period, in both young and old metropolitan areas. More important for urban policy is the absolute decline in the central city population in older major metropolitan areas. Table 5.5 shows that the 18 oldest central cities lost over a million residents in the 20-year period after 1950. Despite the decline relative to the suburban ring between 1950 and 1970, the population in central cities of younger and less densely

TABLE 5.5 Changes in central city population for major metropolitan areas, by age, 1950–1970 (in thousands)

	Young SMSAs			Old SMSAs		
	Central city	SMSA	CC/SMSA[a]	Central city	SMSA	CC/SMSA[a]
1950	7,603	12,866	59	27,175	39,817	68
1970	11,747	24,667	48	25,989	59,707	44
Change	4,145	11,801	35	−1,187	19,890	−6
Percentage Change	55	92		−4	50	

[a] Central cities as percentages of SMSAs.
SOURCES: U.S. Bureau of the Census, *1950 Census of Population, State Reports,* and *1970 Census of Population, Advance Report* (PC [VI]–1, January 1971).

populated metropolitan areas increased by 55 percent. Economic pull, social push, and demographic factors are three basic forces that underlie the current flight from the older central cities to the suburbs.

An important economic factor that attracts central city residents to the suburbs is rising income. People generally prefer new housing to old, and affluence is likely to encourage residence in a modern dwelling, most easily found in the suburban ring where open land is available. On the basis of current population and income trends, some observers conclude that the rapid decline of the high-density central city is a product of a high income elasticity of demand for single family dwelling units. Reinforcing this tendency are provisions in the federal income tax law that in effect subsidize the ownership of single family dwellings.[15] Because such housing units are land intensive, they are found almost exclusively in suburban areas where land prices are relatively low. Although there is some truth in this widely accepted explanation of central city decline, it is too narrow because it ignores many other important factors influencing residential location.

A second economic force increasing the attractiveness of suburban living is the rapid rise of employment opportunities on the fringe of major metropolitan areas. This changing distribution of jobs has meant that heads of households could, at the same time, live in proximity to their place of employment and in an area with low population density. This possibility is in sharp contrast to the traditional location model, which assumes there is a significant trade-off between accessibility to job opportunities and low-density living. The proximity of employment as a determinant of residential location is emphasized by economist John F. Kain: "Manufacturing determines the location decisions of households, not vice versa."[16]

The principal demographic factor likely to influence locational preferences is family size. A head of household may prefer to live close to his place of employment in the central city, but increasing family size may lower the relative importance he places on job accessibility. For example, he may prefer to raise his children in a low-density residential neighborhood with less traffic and more places to play outdoors. In that case the household head will accept a longer work trip in order to improve the environment for his children. This demographic factor is particularly influential when public schools in the central city are noticeably inferior to those in the suburban ring.[17] To the extent people prefer to raise children in an environment with a low population density, a life cycle of location preferences is expected. Families rearing children are likely to prefer suburban living, while couples with no children living at home may find areas of high density more acceptable.

In addition to some families being pulled out of the urban core by the attractions of low-density living, residents are often "pushed" out by social forces. The aging housing, deteriorating public school facilities, and the poverty that characterize many older central cities have driven some middle class residents to the suburbs even though they would prefer to live in a quality high-density area if it were available. An important source of this push may be the high crime rates in the central city. Crimes against property occur 1.23 times more frequently in cities with population exceeding 250,000 than in suburban areas, while violent crimes are 4.3 times more numerous.[18] The higher risk of being victimized by crime in the central city is apt to cause some people to seek residence in the more wealthy suburban enclaves.

Economic and social forces that account for the popularity of suburban residential locations operate selectively. Poor families are unable to move out of the central city because they cannot afford the new housing that is typically found on the urban fringe. In the case of blacks, residential discrimination compounds the difficulties. As indicated in Chapter 3, this segregation may perpetuate the poverty that is in part responsible for the decline of the central city.

Poverty in the central city is a major cause of the social push and demographic factors that increase the desirability of a suburban residence. Any flight by the middle class to the urban fringe further reduces the viability of the central city as a place of residence for that group. As relatively high-income households vacate the central city, those remaining have more contact with the poor and less with middle class peers. The increasing impoverishment of the central city intensifies the force of social push for the remaining middle class families. This vicious cycle continues to push affluent families to the suburbs and perpetuates the decline of the central city.

THE FUTURE OF THE CENTRAL CITY

Whether or not the central city is worth saving depends on the degree of homogeneity we are willing to accept in our metropolitan areas. Central cities in new metropolitan areas have realized increases in economic activity in part because they are indistinguishable from the suburban ring in older metropolitan areas. Their urban form is based on the automobile and truck transportation that fosters relatively low population densities. These central cities do not provide consumers with an option for high-density living and thus deprive them of an economy of scale in consumption that can be offered by cities.

Absolute decline of central cities in older metropolitan areas and the homogeneity of new urban areas suggest that the traditional central city may not be a viable location for economic activity. The decay process that is currently ruling older central city fortunes does not necessarily spell the doom of these traditionally high-density urban cores. Many of the massive suburban tracts filled with relatively inexpensive homes will soon be both too old and too poor in quality to suit their current occupants. As the central city is renewed, it may possess new housing and accessibility to jobs, a combination previously enjoyed by residents of suburban areas.

The central city will be renewed. As buildings decay and as poverty declines, increasing portions of the city will be redeveloped for new purposes. A key issue facing urban policy makers is the nature of this renewal. Observing the decline in central city economic activity, planners often conclude that a densely populated urban core is obsolete. Permitting the continued decline of these areas for lack of an alternative policy would eliminate retailing activities that require dense populations and would destroy the opportunity for a life style dominated by the interpersonal contact fostered by the traditional urban core. Such a policy would reduce the number of options available to the consumer, while a more desirable alternative would not homogenize the metropolitan area or limit consumer choice.

A projection of past employment and population trends into the future suggests a bleak outlook for the high-density central city as a location for economic activity. In the past 20 years, the 18 older central cities lost over 7 percent of their manufacturing and wholesaling employment as well as 14 percent of their retailing activity. The expansion of the relatively small service sector has been insufficient to offset these losses of employment. Since declining population and employment is likely to reduce the viability of such central city locations, the rate of decline may be accelerated in the future.

Such a forecast, however, may be unnecessarily pessimistic. The proportion of jobs in the United States that is compelled by technology to locate on the fringe of metropolitan areas is declining. As a proportion of the nonagricultural labor force, manufacturing employment fell from 29 percent in 1947 to 27 percent in 1967. Since it is manufacturing technology that is the most land-intensive, a larger proportion of workers could be employed in the central city. Further, many nonproduction workers in manufacturing industries may be technologically free to locate in high-density urban areas. Production workers as a proportion of total manufacturing employment fell from 83 percent in 1947 to a 1967 figure of 76 percent. The proportion of total employment engaged in manufacturing production thus fell from .24 in 1947 to .21 in 1967.

Not only can most office work be located in areas of high density without significantly raising costs, but the workers in office buildings may prefer such a location. A large proportion of the office corps is young and unmarried, a group that tends to enjoy the wide variety of specialty shops and entertainment in the core of the metropolitan area. The central city and its central business district appear to be a viable location for many service and office activities.

If employment in activities that can locate in a traditional central city is increasing, the claimed technological obsolescence of the central city is overstated. That employment in such activities will continue to increase is a basic tenet of the "cybernetic revolution." According to this view, employment in the manufacturing sector will decline because of ever increasing labor productivity that is a result of improved technology. An increasing proportion of the labor force will be engaged in sectors where technology is less easily applied, such as the performing arts, education, fine restaurants, and other leisure time activities. The implications of such uneven technological advance have been analyzed by William Baumol. In the extreme case where labor productivity is constant in one sector and rising exponentially in the other, Baumol shows that an increasing proportion of the labor force will be employed in the technologically unprogressive sector.[19] It is undeniable that technological advance has progressed more rapidly in manufacturing than in other sectors of the economy. The unbalanced growth of technology suggests that the proportion of labor force in nonmanufacturing activities is likely to increase. Since these activities do not require large amounts of land, there is no reason why they could not be located in an area of high density. As a result, claims that the traditional, high-density central city is technologically obsolete are exaggerated.

The future of the traditional, high-density urban core in part depends on the number of people that will find employment in the central city. Increasing employment in nonmanufacturing activities that do not require large amounts of land suggests that areas of high density are viable in the long run. When renewing the central city, urban policy should foster areas of high density so that residents may enjoy a choice between living among many people and the relative isolation of the suburban experience.

EXTERNALITIES AND LAND-USE PATTERNS

Economic and social activity are compressed into a relatively small land area in metropolitan areas. While there are many advantages to this agglomeration of activity, the physical proximity of different functions can also be an important source of negative third-party effects. Zoning is the traditional planning tool used to minimize the externalities that result from physical proximity. A basic function of zoning is to separate activities in order to minimize the number of negative externalities that may reduce the welfare of the population. A manufacturing activity that emits a lot of noise, for example, should not be allowed to locate near a residential development if its occupants would suffer from the noise.[20] Similarly, aesthetic considerations may provide a basis for separating many economic activities from areas of residential location.

Discussions on the appropriate scope and purpose of zoning shed light on the effectiveness of zoning for the control of externalities. One view stresses the importance of protecting the current distribution of private property values:

> Zoning . . . directs new growth into appropriate areas and *protects existing property* [italics mine] by requiring that development afford adequate light, air and privacy for persons living and working within the municipality . . . of major importance for the individual citizen is the part zoning plays in stabilizing and preserving property values.[21]

Justice William O. Douglas delivered an opinion in 1954 that set a broader role for zoning:

> . . . the concept of the public welfare is broad and inclusive . . . the values it represents are spiritual as well as physical, aesthetic as well as monetary. It is within the power of the legislature to determine that the community should be beautiful as well as healthy, spacious as well as clean, well balanced as well as carefully patrolled.[22]

Some economists would argue that the apparent differences between these two positions are greater than the real differences because negative externalities are reflected in property values. When a business firm locates in a residential neighborhood, property values will fall if the area becomes a less desirable place to live. Thus, protecting the healthfulness and the aesthetic aspects of a neighborhood will also prevent a reduction in the value of property.

There remains, however, a critical distinction between the narrow, property-value approach to zoning and the broader scope suggested by Justice Douglas. Zoning that is designed to protect property values is likely to distribute the benefits to the owners of property rather than the community at large. The potential conflict between the public interest and property values is easily demonstrated. If an apartment complex does not provide enough off-street parking for its residents, the public must provide on-street parking for them. Not providing off-street parking lowers the cost to the private developer, thus raising the net present value of his project and increasing the value of his property. This is clearly a negative externality to the public at large, which, in providing on-street parking, is subsidizing a residential development. An important role of zoning is to prevent negative externalities that some owners of property might inflict on the rest of society.

Because property values can be influenced by zoning, owners of property take particular interest in legislation that affects land-use patterns. Interests of the society at large, however, are likely to be under-represented in discussions affecting zoning policy because poor and middle class families do not own enough property to merit active participation in the development of land-use policies. Large property owners, on the other hand, have a substantial interest in policies that may affect property values. Because of this interest, large property owners are likely to wield a disproportionate amount of influence in the local political arena, a fact that may explain the preoccupation of zoning with the protection of property values. Zoning ordinances are therefore likely to reflect the active interests of the few large landowners rather than the communitywide interests that provide small benefits to a large number of people.

In the interests of maintaining the property values of suburban communities, some local governments have passed zoning legislation that is designed to perpetuate income segregation in the metropolitan area.

The mechanism is deceptively simple. The citizens inside the fortress simply declare that "in the interest of community, health, welfare, and general security," each new applicant for admission must be required to purchase and build one single family home on one or three or ten acres of land. Or they may simply declare that garden apartments or row houses are *ipso facto* detrimental and bar them altogether, even if surrounded by 100 acres of open land. There are no standards to govern such zoning.[23]

Such zoning legislation makes it more difficult for the poor to leave the central city and move to suburban areas, where the number of job opportunities is growing rapidly. This lack of mobility frustrates the urban upgrading function and as a result helps maintain the blight and poverty that characterize large portions of many central cities. Segrega-

tion by income class is one way land-use patterns in one political jurisdiction can have an adverse affect on other communities in the metropolitan area. This phenomenon of multiple political jurisdictions in
metropolitan areas, called *fiscal fragmentation,* is analyzed in detail in
Chapter 8.

Land use and environmental pollution

From its inception, zoning has regulated the location of industries that
give rise to negative externalities. In 1916 the City of New York passed
its first zoning ordinance for the purpose of barring these "nuisance
industries" from many parts of the city. These industries are responsible
for such negative externalities as noxious odors, air and water pollution,
and excessive noise. Edgar Hoover and Raymond Vernon estimated
that in 1956 more than one in five manufacturing workers were employed in nuisance industries in the New York SMSA.[24] Many firms
engaged in meat processing, petroleum refining, and metal refining as
well as in the production of chemicals, fertilizers, and rubber goods,
were identified as nuisance industries. Industrial polluters undoubtedly
contribute to the current environmental problems that are becoming
of increasing concern.

Isolating polluters of air and water resources via zoning ordinances
may reduce their adverse impact on the community. However, such
legislation does not deal with the issue of environmental pollution.
Requiring the polluter of a river to locate on the downstream side of
the metropolitan area protects residents from the pollution but lowers
the quality of water in regions further downstream. Zoning regulates
the use of land in a metropolitan area without regard to regional or
national interests. As such, local zoning legislation has in effect sanc-
tioned the pollution of public resources such as air and water. Polluters
of the environment must be controlled by legislation designed to protect air and water resources, not by legislation designed to foster efficient land use within a particular metropolitan area.

Shaping land use through zoning is not an effective way to change
basic location patterns in our major metropolitan areas. A desirable use
of urban land can be facilitated by the elimination of some problems
that are best solved by the federal government. Concentrations of poor
families in central cities is an important cause for the flight of the middle
class to suburban areas. An effective antipoverty program would
reduce this element in residential location decisions, and families would
be freer to choose a neighborhood because of its physical properties
rather than its income composition. The following chapters indicate
that location trends are also closely related to developments in housing
and transportation.

NOTES

[1] William Alonso, "Cities, Planners, and Urban Renewal," in James Q. Wilson, ed., *Urban Renewal: The Record and the Controversy* (Cambridge: M.I.T. Press, 1966), pp. 449, 452.

[2] Norton E. Long, "Local Government and Renewal Policies," in James. Q. Wilson, ed., op.cit., pp. 422–423.

[3] In smaller metropolitan areas the relationship between density and population growth in the central city is less clear. The population in many of these areas is slow growing because of a slow expansion of employment opportunities in the region. The Wilkes-Barre metropolitan area, located in the depressed coal-producing region of Pennsylvania, actually lost population between 1950 and 1970. In the case of smaller SMSAs, factors affecting regional economic development are likely to be more important in determining the growth of the central city than population density.

[4] William Alonso, op. cit., p. 450.

[5] This advantage of living in an area of high density is clearly neutralized when consumers feel that streets are not safe at night. High crime rates, therefore, undermine the advantages of central city living and contribute to their decline.

[6] Leon Moses and Harold F. Williamson, Jr., "The Location of Economic Activity in Cities," *American Economic Review*, 52: (May 1967) 211–222.

[7] Formulations typically assume that a fixed budget (K) is allocated between transportation costs (T, including both direct travel costs and the monetary equivalent of time and discomfort) and location rent (R). That is $k = T + R$ and $R = K - T$. See Richard F. Muth, "Urban Residential Land and Housing Markets," in H. Perloff and L. Wingo, eds., *Issues in Urban Economics* (Baltimore: Johns Hopkins Press, 1968), and Lowdon Wingo, *Transportation and Urban Land* (Washington, D.C.: Resources for the Future, 1961).

[8] See Edgar M. Hoover, *The Location of Economic Activity* (New York: McGraw-Hill, 1948), ch. 6.

[9] For both international and historical comparisons of the rent gradient, see Colin Clark, *Population Growth and Land Use* (New York: St. Martin, 1967), ch. 9.

[10] All manufacturing activity is frequently included in the economic base of a region. These export activities provide earnings with which residents of an area can purchase services which are called nonbasic activities. For a more detailed description of the basic-nonbasic dichotomy, see E. M. Hoover, *An Introduction to Regional Economics* (New York: Knopf, 1971), ch. 8.

[11] It should be noted that the demand curve could be downward sloping, i.e., not perfectly elastic, and not change the basic argument.

[12] Edgar M. Hoover and Raymond Vernon, *Anatomy of a Metropolis* (Garden City, N.Y.: Doubleday, 1962), pp. 59–60.

[13] This relationship may be stated formally in a gravity model. The frequency of interaction between consumer i and retailer j (F_{ij}) will be positively related to the attractiveness of the retail operation (A_j) and affected inversely by the retailer's distance from the consumer (d_{ij}). Mathematically, $F_{ij} = K(A_{ij}^a / d_{ij}^b)$ where K, a, and b are parameters that generalize the model so a specific relationship between the variables is not implied. See W. Isard et al., *Methods of Regional Analysis* (Cambridge: M.I.T. Press, 1960), ch. 11.

[14] These cities are Baltimore, New Orleans, New York, Philadelphia, Saint Louis, San Francisco, and Washington, D.C. The data are found in U.S. Department of Commerce, Bureau of the Census, *County Business Patterns*, 1948 and 1967.

[15] This is explained in detail in Chapter 6, "Housing and Urban Renewal."

[16] John F. Kain, "The Distribution and Movement of Jobs and Industry," in James Q. Wilson, ed., *The Metropolitan Enigma* (Cambridge: Harvard University Press, 1968), p. 17.

[17] The phenomenon of unequal public services between municipalities in metropolitan areas is discussed in Chapter 8, "The Urban Public Sector."

[18] *HUD Statistical Yearbook* (Washington, D.C.: Government Printing Office, 1969), pp. 348–349. The violent crime rate in SMSAs is 416.6 per 100,000 population compared to 162.6 for suburban areas. The crime against property rate is 2679.3 for SMSAs while it is only 1778.2 in the suburban fringe.

[19] William J. Baumol, "Macroeconomics of Unbalanced Growth: The Anatomy of Urban Crisis," *American Economic Review* 57 (June 1967): 415–426.

[20] Many economists suggest that this problem may be handled by having either the firm pay the residents to put up with the noise or the residents pay the firm to locate elsewhere. If the world worked so perfectly, of course, there would be no need for zoning.

[21] William L. Goodman, ed., *Principles and Practice of Urban Planning* (Washington, D.C.: International City Managers Association, 1968), p. 403.

[22] *Berman* v. *Parker,* in Goodman, ed., op. cit., pp. 403–404.

[23] Clarence Funnye, "Zoning: The New Battleground," *Architectural Forum,* May 1970, p. 63.

[24] Hoover and Vernon, op. cit., p. 72.

RECOMMENDED READINGS

Birch, David L. *The Economic Future of City and Suburb.* Committee of Economic Development, Supplementary Paper No. 30, 1970.

Funnye, Clarence. "Zoning: The New Battleground," *Architectural Forum,* May 1970.

Goldberg, Michael A. "Transportation, Urban Land Values and Rent: A Synthesis," *Land Economics,* May 1970. Reprinted in D. W. Rasmussen and C. T. Haworth, eds., *The Modern City: A Book of Readings.* New York: Harper & Row, 1973.

Hoover, Edgar M. *The Location of Economic Activity.* New York: McGraw-Hill, 1948, ch. 6.

Hoover, Edgar M. and Raymond Vernon, *Anatomy of a Metropolis.* Garden City, N.Y. Doubleday, 1962.

Kain, John F. "The Distribution and Movement of Jobs and Industry," in James Q. Wilson, ed., *The Metropolitan Enigma.* Cambridge: Harvard University Press, 1968.

Moses, Leon and Williamson, Harold F. "The Location of Economic Activity in Cities," *American Economic Review,* May 1967.

Sternlieb, George. "The City as Sandbox," *Public Interest,* Fall 1971. Reprinted in Rasmussen and Haworth, op. cit.

Tiebout, Charles. "Intra-Urban Location Problems: An Evaluation," *American Economic Review,* May 1961.

6
HOUSING
AND URBAN RENEWAL

Housing plays an important role in determining the location of residences and the decline of the central city. Middle class residents leave the central city for the suburban fringe in part because of their demand for modern housing. As argued in the preceding chapter, the concentration of poor households in low-quality housing hastens the decline of the central city by "pushing" higher-income groups to suburban enclaves. To the extent that the distribution of high-quality housing is responsible for this segregation of the poor, it may be frustrating the city's upgrading function. Aspects of housing that affect those with relatively low socioeconomic status are analyzed in this chapter.

Urban blight, slums, and overcrowded dwellings are not the only issues associated with housing policy. High-income middle class families have an interest in being able to choose between houses with different physical layouts and architectural styles at various population densities. Consumer satisfaction is higher when this choice is available. Effective consumer choice among housing types is essential if the metropolitan area is to offer the economies of scale in consumption that are an important function of major urban settlements. Housing policy affects the welfare of higher-income groups as well as that of the poor. To clarify the issues associated with public policy in this area, the nature of housing services must be analyzed.

THE NATURE OF HOUSING

Public policy in the United States has long recognized the importance of housing in human welfare. In 1949 a Housing Act stated: "The

general welfare and security of the nation . . . require . . . the realization, as soon as possible, of the goal of a decent home and suitable
living environment for every American family."[1] The phrase "suitable
living environment" suggests that our housing policy is founded on the
premise that housing is more than mere shelter. A bewildering array of
economic, psychological, and sociological phenomena surround housing problems and must be clarified if a rational housing policy is to be
realized.

Good housing may be a prerequisite for the smooth operation of a
modern society. Abraham Maslow has argued that man has a hierarchy
of needs, extending from the most basic physiological needs, such as
food, to the higher order needs of "self-actualization" (realizing one's
full potential) and aesthetic experience.[2] Basic needs must be satisfied
before people desire higher order needs—a starving man is not preoccupied with realizing his full potential. If the need for safety and security
is closely related to the quality of living environment, good housing is
a prerequisite for realizing one's full potential. Living in a badly dilapidated, rat-infested slum could easily reinforce any pessimistic assessment of the future that the poor hold. Alvin Schorr has stated, ". . . the
evidence is overwhelming: *extremely poor* housing conditions percep-
tibly influence behavior and attitudes."[3] Improving the housing of the
very poor should help break the failure syndrome, which keeps some
poor persons in the vicious cycle of poverty. Better housing not only
improves the well-being of the poor, but it may also enhance the city's
capacity to absorb the poor into modern economic life.

A suitable living environment is widely accepted as an important goal
for public policy. The components of such an environment, however,
are less clear. Housing is frequently discussed in terms of the "dwelling
unit"—shelter defined independently of its surroundings—the quality
of which can be measured in such physical terms as the presence of
plumbing or central heating. Although the importance of the dwelling
unit should not be minimized when assessing housing quality, recent
research suggests that, in many cases, other aspects are just as important. Housing means more than a dwelling unit: It also includes the
physical surroundings or neighborhood in which the unit is located.

The welding of private shelters and public streets into neighborhoods
offering a high-quality living environment is a concept given classic
expression by Jane Jacobs. By emphasizing the use of sidewalks to
promote safety, contact, and the socialization of children, Jacobs
makes a strong case for combining individual dwelling units into larger
geographic units to enhance the well-being of the residents.[4] People
at their daily tasks on the sidewalks are "eyes on the street" that supervise the play of children and provide mutual protection. These neighborhoods also provide residents with a sense of community—a combi-

nation of people and physical structures with which they can identify.

Psychological and sociological studies of residents of relatively poor housing confirm that a suitable living environment includes more than shelter of reasonable quality. In fact, some of the work suggests that the quality of shelter is in some cases less important than the neighborhood in which it is located. Edward Ryan's study of the West End of Boston indicates that this area of low-quality housing was characterized by friendly and personalized relations between its residents.

> It was impressive how infrequently the question of "what is his occupation?" was asked. It was also not common, in referring to another person, to specify his occupation. This information was not a critical element in the placing of another person . . . another person was more likely to be placed and talked about relative to his moral characteristics and his sociability.[5]

Put another way:

> The people never idealized their housing itself. What they did value was the combination of type of building and setting of buildings relative to each other, the streets, and the commercial land use. This combination brought people into frequent, spontaneous contact with their relatives. It strongly supported their life style.[6]

On the basis of interviews conducted in the same area, Fried and Gleicher concluded that West End residents received satisfaction from their identity with the street and that the home is not merely an apartment or other dwelling unit.[7] After renewal of the West End, Fried found that many dislocated residents expressed feelings of grief over the loss of this environment.[8]

West-Enders in Boston and residents of the type of neighborhood envisioned by Jacobs have a spatial identity that exceeds the boundaries of their individual dwelling unit. Persons in these communities have a relatively high proportion of their contacts with people living in the immediate area. This life-style is the classic tribal arrangement, where the bulk of the society lives and works in a relatively small geographic area. Communication within such a social organization is often spontaneous, based on chance meetings in the street or other public places. The relevant physical environment for such a community consists of the type, size, and spatial arrangement of the neighborhood as well as the quality of the individual shelter.

In contrast to the close physical proximity of residents in classical tribal societies and some urban neighborhoods, modern suburban living is characterized by the geographical isolation of individuals. Because of the significant distances between dwellings of friends, all attempts at communication must be premeditated. When the automobile provides all people with individualized transportation, there are fewer public places where neighbors are likely to meet. Residents of such an environment identify not with their neighbors but with people in other parts of the city with whom they share work or some other interest. Automobiles introduce flexibility and speed into the urban transportation system but at the cost of undermining the sense of community among neighbors. Informal contact with neighbors is not an important aspect of life under the mobile form of social organization typical of the modern city. When the sense of community among residents of an area is minimal, the individual dwelling unit is clearly the dominant feature determining housing quality.

There are two issues connected with housing that are of concern to the urban economist. The first deals with the quality of housing in a metropolitan area, with particular reference to those units in which the poor reside. The second concerns the range of different kinds of dwellings and neighborhoods available to families; this is important if residents of a metropolitan area are to enjoy economies of scale in the consumption of housing.

An important aspect of urban public policy is the role of housing in assimilating the poor into the mainstream of American life. As already noted, extremely dilapidated shelter can inhibit the desire for individual improvement, a cornerstone of public efforts to increase the socioeconomic status of the poorest members of society. Another aspect of the upgrading function in urban areas is suggested by the hypothesis that housing is more than shelter. The supervision of children required for their socialization as well as safety is most easily accomplished in low-rise residences, where the parents are, at most, only a few flights from the ground. Rearing children is complicated in high-rise apartment dwellings, since parents cannot supervise their offspring when they are on the street many stories below and it is often neither practical nor desirable for children to remain indoors. This assimilation of children is fostered in the neighborhoods envisioned by Jane Jacobs.

> . . . on lively diversified sidewalks they [people of cities] do supervise the incidental play of children and assimilate the children into city society. They do it in the course of carrying on their other pursuits.
>
> Planners do not seem to realize how high a ratio of adults is needed to rear children at incidental play. Nor do they seem to understand that spaces and equipment do not rear children. These can be useful adjuncts, but only people rear children and assimilate them into civilized society.[9]

Housing can be used to help upgrade the poor and introduce them to the societal norms of middle class behavior. Viewed in this utilitarian way, policy attempts to improve housing quality should be evaluated by their effectiveness in changing the life style of poor families. This manipulation of most poor families is unnecessary because they already hold middle class values. Although fostering this socialization process is a valid objective of policy, the increase in the welfare of the poor as a result of improved housing is sufficient to merit public action designed to improve the quality of the housing stock.

While socioeconomic improvement is most important for the poor, the provision of a choice between alternative life styles is the most important aspect of housing policy for the relatively wealthy members of society. Various authors have analyzed the merits of high-density living near the urban core relative to low-density suburban living.[10] This research suggests that there is no a priori case for the superiority of one life style over the other. Facilitating an effective choice between them would probably improve the welfare of the middle class population and therefore should be incorporated into urban housing policy. Aspects of housing quality are discussed before we turn to methods of improving the quality of housing in urban areas.

THREE ASPECTS OF HOUSING QUALITY

A standard dwelling unit has been typically defined in terms of the physical condition of the housing and the availability of basic plumbing facilities. Minimum acceptable standards require that a dwelling is not dilapidated and has hot running water, a flush toilet, and a bathtub or shower for the private use of the household.[11] Using this somewhat narrow physical criterion of quality in the housing stock, the trends show a dramatic decline in the number of substandard dwellings in metropolitan areas. The number of families living in substandard housing in the United States fell from 14.6 million in 1950 to 4.7 million in 1970. This reduction of 9.9 million substandard units represents a decline from 32 percent of the total in 1950 to 7 percent in 1970.

Improvements in the housing stock are usually assumed to represent a net increase in the economic welfare of the society. The relationship between changes in the quality of housing and consumer welfare is complicated by the presence of two other variables: the incidence of overcrowding and the proportion of income spent on housing. This is shown in Figure 6.1. Given the supply (SS) and demand (DD) for inexpensive housing shown in this figure, the market price for these housing services is p_o for q_o quantity. If, for example, government policy on housing standards forces consumers to purchase a larger quantity of housing (q), it will be provided by the private sector only at price p. However, given the demand (DD) for this housing, consumers are willing to pay only p_1 for this required amount of housing. Consumer demands for dwellings smaller than q are negated by this policy, and

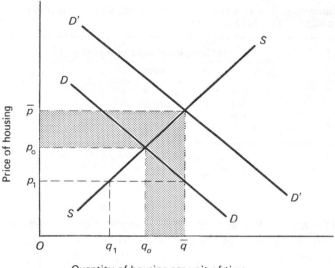

FIGURE 6.1. Changes in housing quality and consumer welfare.

households must now increase their expenditures for housing by the amount of the shaded area. This increase in expenditure may be achieved at the opportunity cost of spending less on other items, which, for low-income families, may be badly needed food, clothing, or medical care. Alternatively, this increase in cost may be covered by having another family share the expenses, by overcrowding the dwelling unit. In this event, of course, a family may actually spend less on housing than before but will consume fewer housing services. Improved housing may be financed by one of these two methods that raise the effective demand for housing from DD to $D'D'$. Evaluation of the impact of improvements in the housing stock on the welfare of the population should therefore include the incidence of overcrowding and the proportion of income spent on housing.

In the United States a dwelling is considered overcrowded when it houses more than one person per room. The incidence of overcrowding in metropolitan areas fell markedly from 1950 to 1970. In the former year, over 13 percent of all dwellings were overcrowded compared to 8 percent in the latter year; this trend indicates that improvements in the housing quality were not financed by an increase in overcrowding of dwelling units.

Table 6.1 shows that all income classes spent more for housing in 1970 than they did in 1960. Although comparable data for 1950 are not available, other comparisons suggest that income spent on housing

TABLE 6.1 Median percentage of income spent on rental housing, by income level for metropolitan areas, 1960 and 1970

Income level	Median percentage of income		
	1960	1970	Change
0–4,999	30.0	35.0	5
5,000–9,999	15.0	19.9	4.9
10,000–14,999	10.6	14.4	3.8
over 15,000	less than 10.0	11.0	more than 1

SOURCE: Estimated from *1960 Census of Housing, Metropolitan Housing,* Table B-3 and from *1970 Census of Population and Housing, Census Tracts* (Washington, D.C.: Government Printing Office, 1963 and 1972).

rose between 1950 and 1960 as well. The proportion of households spending more than 20 percent of their income on rent increased for every income level reported—in five of seven cases the increase was 150 percent or greater. Substantial increases in the cost of housing as a proportion of income raises doubt that consumer welfare increased as a result of improved housing quality. Since people paid more for their housing services, the decline in the number of substandard dwellings may not raise consumer welfare. Increasing housing costs could be the price of flight from the central city and the problems caused by the large concentration of low-income families in that portion of many major metropolitan areas. Deterioration of old neighborhoods may force middle class families to the suburban ring in order to avoid a decline in overall housing quality. If these factors force otherwise satisfied central city residents to move into higher-priced suburban housing, the decline in welfare is clear. An increase in the demand for housing relative to its supply would make consumers worse off by forcing them to pay a higher price for housing. Migration to metropolitan areas and an increase in the formation of new households due to the maturation of babies born after World War II have swelled the demand for housing. However, if these increases in expenditures on housing reflect a change in consumer tastes for housing, consumer welfare has not been diminished. To the extent they were forced on households by socioeconomic forces, the reduction in the number of substandard dwellings exaggerates the increase in consumer welfare.

Increases in the cost of housing are particularly burdensome for low-income households. Of every 100 households with an income below $5,000 in 1970, 67 spent over 35 percent of it on housing services. By comparison, virtually none of the households with an annual income exceeding $15,000 spent this much on shelter. While it is not surprising that low-income families spend more of their resources on necessities such as housing, it is clear that any public or private action that raises the cost of life's necessities is a cruel tax on the poor. Programs that lower the supply of low-quality housing when demand remains unchanged raise the cost of shelter to the poor. By reducing the supply of food through a system of farm price supports, the federal government has raised the price of this necessity.[12] Housing programs designed to improve the quality of dwelling units must be carefully conceived if they are not to duplicate the regressive tax imposed by our agricultural policies.

STRATEGIES FOR IMPROVING THE HOUSING STOCK

Strategies to improve the housing stock must be evaluated in terms of their impact on the relative cost of housing as well as their effect on housing quality. Society's desire to place low-income families in better homes must be tempered by recognition of the other claims upon the meager resources of the poor. Furthermore, increases in housing quality should not be gained at the expense of a reduction in consumer choice. It is in this latter respect that the more affluent members of society have a vested interest in the operation of housing programs. Four strategies for improving the housing stock are analyzed below: (1) conservation and rehabilitation; (2) urban renewal and public housing; (3) filtering; and (4) income supplements.

Conservation and rehabilitation

Most obvious of strategies to increase the quality of housing is to reduce the rate of decay of residences and improve low-quality units. The use of many older buildings is made possible by the generally high quality of their construction and continued maintenance. Conserving and rehabilitating single and multifamily dwellings is becoming increasingly popular in many high-density central cities. Reclamation of central city housing for use by the middle class fosters choice of life styles by maintaining the physical structure of traditional neighborhoods in some sections of the metropolitan area. Destruction of these areas often reduces the number of traditional neighborhoods in the city, because urban renewal rarely replaces the low-rise multifamily housing units that are destroyed.

Conservation and rehabilitation are attractive as a tool of housing policy because they reduce the need for new dwellings and foster the maintenance of a traditional urban life style. However, maintenance of high-density neighborhoods is sometimes frustrated by uncertainties in the private market mechanism. These uncertainties create a divergence between private and public interests and are a product of the interdependence of property values. One problem uncertainty creates has been analyzed in the context of the "Prisoner's Dilemma."[13] When an aging neighborhood is threatened by blight, owners of real estate are faced with the options of either maintaining and improving their property or permitting the area to decay. Because the value of property is in large part determined by the condition of the surrounding area, the decision of a property owner is influenced by what he *thinks* will be the response of his neighbors. If an individual rehabilitates his property while his neighbors fail to do so, the increase in the value of his property will be modest because the improved property is surrounded by blight and continuing decay.

Hypothetical rates of return on property improvement in Table 6.2 show how the rate of return on property improvement can be affected by the actions of others in a blighted neighborhood. If owners do not maintain their property, we assume that their investable funds would be left in a savings account. Hence, in the two-household neighborhood of Table 6.2, when neither owner maintains his property, each receives a 5 percent rate of return. If both owners invest, the higher property values in the neighborhood caused by the improvements may yield a higher rate of return to each owner, e.g., 10 percent.[14] If only one property owner invests, his rate of return may be as low as 3 percent, while the noninvestor enjoys a modest windfall gain. The noninvestor receives what may be called an infinite rate of return, since the value of his property increases at no cost to himself.

Variations in the rate of return shown in Table 6.2 indicate why the market mechanism inadvertently discourages the conservation and rehabilitation of blighted and/or deteriorating neighborhoods. Unlike "healthy" residential areas, such places are characterized by owners who believe their neighbors will not invest in property improvements. Given the expectation that others will not invest, a property owner is faced with the following choice: to invest in property improvement and probably receive only a 3 percent rate of return, or not to invest and receive 5 percent. If he does not invest, his lowest rate of return will

TABLE 6.2 Hypothetical rates of return on housing improvements for two property owners in a blighted neighborhood

Owners investing		Rate of return	
Owner I	Owner II	Owner I	Owner II
YES	YES	.10	.10
YES	NO	.03	—
NO	YES	—	.03
NO	NO	.05	.05

be 5 percent and the largest infinite, while investing will yield a low of 3 and a high of 10 percent. In the uncertain atmosphere of a blighted residential area, the rational investor will not improve his property, and neighborhood decline will continue unabated.

The Prisoner's Dilemma can be resolved only if the principals cooperate to reduce the level of uncertainty. If all members of the community are motivated to maximize their rate of return in the short run, even neighborhood organization will not resolve the problem inasmuch as noninvestors are likely to receive a greater return than investors. While such efforts may succeed where owners feel a vested interest in the stability of the neighborhood, the high mobility of many urban residents undermines their willingness to cooperate. Nonresident owners in a neighborhood also reduce the chance for property improvement, since they are not likely to identify with a community in which their only interest is financial.

Even if residents of a blighted neighborhood decide to rehabilitate their residences, they may not be able to borrow the funds to finance the improvements. Jane Jacobs has described a banker's prejudice against Boston's North End: "No sense in lending money into the North End . . . it's a slum . . . back in the depression it had a very large number of foreclosures; bad record."[15] The banker cites his experience of several decades earlier to condemn a neighborhood to a process of continuing decay.

The difficulty of insuring property in blighted areas compounds the obstacles to improving the existing housing supply. The following exchange between a Boston realtor and former Senator Paul Douglas illustrates the problem:

MR. ROMANOS   As far as apartment house property, it is practically impossible to get insurance. The only way I get some insurance is I couple it with a building in another area and say "If you want this particular building, then you'll have to take this other one with it."

MR. DOUGLAS   What are the reasons which insurance companies give for not insuring?

MR. ROMANOS   Roxbury—just Roxbury, the area. And now the area is spread from Roxbury to the South End and North Dorchester and certain parts of Jamaica Plain. Originally they had what they call a "red-line" area. They never admitted to the red-line area but they had maps with a red line going around it.[16]

The Prisoner's Dilemma and limited access to capital markets and insurance are not the only barriers to the conservation and rehabilitation of neighborhoods on the verge of becoming blighted. Reliance on the property tax as a source of local revenue reduces the incentive to improve the existing housing stock. Disincentives are particularly strong for blighted neighborhoods in central cities because the tax rate is frequently highest in this portion of metropolitan areas. As a result of its aging physical structures and relatively low-income population, the central city has more problems than the newer and more efficient suburbs. In a major study of the property tax, economist Dick Netzer concluded, "Heavy taxation of real property is a deterrent to the rebuilding of the big cities, especially when it is high in relation to the prevailing rates in the suburbs."[17] Improvements in housing that raise the market value of the property also raise the tax burden. Although the property is worth more, the annual cost of residing in the improved dwelling rises; this may be a significant barrier to rehabilitating housing owned by low-income residents.[18]

Conservation and rehabilitation of older dwellings play an important role in housing policy. For most residential areas, conservation of housing is a normal process subject to none of the barriers mentioned above. Rehabilitating blighted areas is an effective way to maintain the consumer's option for living in traditional high-density neighborhoods. The increasing popularity of rehabilitated central city housing among the middle class suggests that this is an important aspect of public policy. Effective conservation in deteriorating neighborhoods is unlikely, because of the interdependence of decisions made in the private sector. The Prisoner's Dilemma may discourage many investors, while insurance and banking institutions are apt to raise further barriers to those undaunted by the unwillingness of their neighbors to invest. Once people *think* blight is inevitable in a neighborhood, the reluctance to invest in the area soon makes it more blighted, culminating in a dynamic deterioration that leads to the eventual destruction of the area.

In many cases only public action can overcome the inertia of both owners and private financial institutions. Publicly funded and staffed neighborhood-redevelopment organizations may help to overcome the hesitance to invest that stems from the Prisoner's Dilemma. Nonprofit organizations such as community development corporations are required if near-blighted neighborhoods are to break the process of deterioration caused by attempts to maximize personal economic gain without reference to the interdependence of these decisions. Such organizations can also facilitate the involvement of private financial institutions in the rehabilitation of blighted housing.

Urban renewal and public housing

In the short run, elimination of blighted areas through their renewal or reconstruction is a strategy that improves housing quality. Physical removal of urban blight has all too often in the past been substituted for solution of the problem. Families with low income require inexpensive housing; they buy or rent blighted housing because it is cheap, not because they prefer it on its own merits. Typical urban renewal projects improve the average quality of housing by destroying substandard dwellings but nonetheless make poor households worse off. Since the advent of an urban renewal project is unlikely to increase the income of poor persons, the demand for inexpensive housing will probably not be changed by the project. Given the demand curve (DD) in Figure 6.2, the destruction of blighted housing by urban renewal can be illustrated by the shift in supply from SS to $S'S'$. After the upgrading of the housing stock, the poor pay more (p_2-p_1) for less housing (q_1-q_2).[19]

Improvements in the quality of housing generated by urban renewal are apt to be short lived. Owners of near-blighted housing can profit by renting their property to low-income households, particularly if maintenance costs are reduced. Since more substandard housing is created by this process, the number of substandard dwelling units may not be reduced in the long run by the urban renewal project. On the basis of his theoretical analysis of the housing market, Edgar Olsen argues that slum clearance and urban renewal merely shift the location of slums rather than reduce their number if the housing market is perfectly competitive.[20] If the market is not perfectly competitive and the

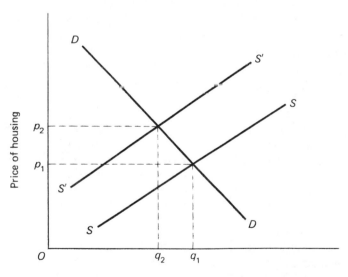

FIGURE 6.2. The effect of urban renewal on the low-income housing market.

supply of housing is inelastic, the poor are likely to pay higher rents for fewer housing services in the long run. These higher rents could be paid if low-income families spent a larger portion of their income on housing, or through overcrowding. Whether or not the housing market is competitive, the efficacy of urban renewal as a strategy to improve the quality of housing is suspect.[21]

Urban renewal often destroys neighborhoods while eliminating blighted and therefore low-income housing. The research on Boston's West End cited earlier in this chapter presents substantial evidence on this score. Neighborhood-oriented business concerns often failed when required by urban renewal to relocate.[22] These small businesses are an integral part of the concept of neighborhood suggested by Jane Jacobs in her *The Death and Life of Great American Cities*. Residents who are on the street to patronize neighborhood businesses provide the eyes that make the street safe and help assimilate children while facilitating contact between neighbors. Elimination of local area shops weakens the fabric that ties individual residences into a geographic entity.

Properly conceived subsidized public housing could offset the declining supply of low-income housing without frustrating the development of a sense of community in such projects. Unfortunately, public housing has all too often created high-rise institutionalized slums that the residents consider undesirable and unsafe. A most dramatic failure of public housing was the massive Pruitt-Igoe project in Saint Louis, which became an unmanageable wasteland a mere 15 years after its construction. These projects provide poor housing in the larger context, despite the fact that the individual units are initially standard dwellings. In testimony before the National Commission on Urban Problems, urban affairs expert Edward J. Logue called public housing "our most significant failure."

> I think you should visit London County Council Housing Estates, where they have shown this can be done. You will always find at the center of each housing project a school, a green grocer, a library, a chemist, a branch bank, and somehow or other a pub. Imagine putting a pub in the middle of that mile of public housing in Chicago; imagine putting a pub out at Columbia Point! But what we are saying, instead, is that 2,500 families in Columbia Point either don't drink or shouldn't. That is a kind of public arrogance which is really unforgivable.[23]

Designing public housing projects to provide standard dwelling units rather than attempting to build a neighborhood may be the root of the failure of urban renewal. Creative design more conducive to the development of a sense of community and a new outlook could make public housing a more valuable component of housing policy.

The fact that urban renewal has often made the poor worse off while attempting to improve the quality of their housing does not imply there is no legitimate role for such policy. If poverty were eliminated from the American scene, the demand for substandard housing would fall dramatically. Renewal of an area for new purposes is justified when blight expands to the point that the price of poor-quality housing is extremely low and/or has a very high vacancy rate.[24] Neighborhoods difficult to rehabilitate or land required for nonresidential purposes (e.g., a sports complex) are potential sites for urban renewal projects that improve the welfare and aesthetic appeal of the entire city.

The supply of low-cost housing can also be effectively reduced by the enforcement of unduly restrictive and outdated building codes that prohibit the use of substandard housing. If these housing codes are enforced, they remove housing from the market as effectively as physical removal. Impoverished households must then either increase the proportion of income spent on shelter or overcrowd a standard dwelling unit. Policies that affect the supply of low-cost housing must be used with caution, for so long as there is a substantial number of households in poverty, there will be a demand for poor housing. Reducing the supply of low-cost housing is, in short, a tax that forces a decrease in welfare for those with the demand for these services.

Filtering

Another strategy to improve housing quality is filtering. When the character of a dwelling unit changes so that its rental value changes, the unit has been "filtered." If maintenance is neglected, the unit deteriorates and is therefore filtered down, while rehabilitation and housing improvements constitute upward filtering. To improve the overall quality of the housing stock, a downward filtering strategy encourages the construction of new housing for upper-income groups. As the new housing is occupied, older dwellings are made available for lower-income groups. If the newly available units are too expensive for the remaining low-income households, they will be filtered down by either subdividing the structures into smaller units or ignoring needed maintenance. A downward filtering strategy will increase the amount of housing available to low-income groups only if the rate of new construction exceeds the rate at which the number of new family units are formed in the area. This approach has appeal because all types of new construction are too expensive for low-income families. The downward filtering mechanism for improving the housing stock has dominated the American housing scene in the post–World War II era.

New construction has been fostered by government programs that make credit more readily available and at lower cost. The Federal Housing Authority (FHA) was formed in order to combat the shortage of credit during the great depression of the 1930s. This program, coupled with various Veterans Administration programs, has influenced private financial institutions to lengthen the repayment period and reduce the down payments required for the purchase of a home. Families must save for long periods of time before they can achieve home ownership when large down payments are required and long-term loans are not available. Policies that reduce the required down payment facilitate the purchase of single family dwellings, a major source of new construction that makes older multifamily dwelling units available for lower-income households.

A principal vehicle for filtering housing to low-income groups is to facilitate new construction. If the price of new housing is reduced relative to that of all other commodities, economic theory suggests that more housing will be purchased. Low-income households would presumably move into the older units vacated by residents of the newly constructed dwellings. A cornerstone of the filtering strategy has been a subsidy to higher-income groups that encourages them to purchase single family dwellings. A provision in the federal income tax law that permits the exclusion of all interest payments from taxable income subsidizes households with income sufficient to purchase a home.[25] Because the income tax is progressive, the higher a family's income, the larger the proportion of interest payments they can deduct. As shown in Table 6.3, the size of the subsidy increases as household income rises. A family with an annual income of $7,500 must pay 32 percent of its income in order to reside in this typical home, while it costs only 4 percent of the resources available to a household with an income of $37,500. This particular aspect of the filtering strategy designed to improve the quality of housing for the poor has the peculiar attribute of subsidizing wealthy families more than those with low incomes.

Earlier in this chapter it was argued that there is no a priori reason to assume that suburban-style single family dwellings are superior to more densely populated "neighborhood" living. Personal preferences determine the relative desirability of these two different life styles. The deduction of interest payments from taxable income, however, suggests that this society has assumed that ownership of a single family dwelling is preferred to living in a rented housing unit. Single family ownership is encouraged by the subsidy because it lowers the cost relative to nonowned housing.[26] Given a set of preferences between any two normal commodities, a reduction in the price of one will result in an increase in its use relative to the good whose price remains unchanged. When the price of home ownership is lowered relative to

TABLE 6.3 Interest subsidy to owners of a "typical" standard home, 1966 (by income level)

Income class (in dollars)	Cost before subsidy[a]	Subsidy[b]	Net cost	cost/income[c]
5,000–10,000	2,492	119	2,373	.32
10,000–15,000	2,492	237	2,255	.18
15,000–25,000	2,492	414	2,078	.10
25,000–50,000	2,492	830	1,660	.04

[a] The cost of standard housing as determined by the Bureau of Labor Statistics for a higher standard of living.
[b] H. Aaron, "Income Taxes and Housing," *American Economic Review* 60 (December 1970), p. 794.
[c] Cost as a percentage of midpoint of the income class.

that of a rental unit, the consumption of the former increases and that of the latter is reduced. This proposition is shown in Figure 6.3. Assume society to be indifferent between the various combinations of quantities of rented and owned housing shown by curve *i*. If all persons spent their housing budget on rental units, they could purchase *OB* units. Similarly, if all housing expenditures were devoted to owned units, *OB'* units could be purchased. The relative prices of the two kinds of housing determine the slope of the budget constraint *BB'*, which shows all the possible combinations of rental and owned housing that can be purchased by the society. The combination Or_1 units of rental housing and Oh_1 owned units maximizes the welfare of the society, because no other combination of housing could move the society to a higher indifference curve. If the price of owned dwellings is subsidized, the slope of the budget constraint will change to, for example, *AB*. Under the new system of relative prices, society will consume more owned units (h_2–h_1) and fewer rental units (r_1–r_2). The population is better off with respect to housing because the subsidy permits society to move to a higher indifference curve (*ii*). Society is not necessarily made better off by this particular improvement in housing because societal welfare must be judged in a broader context.

This distortion of relative prices in the housing market has encouraged the exodus of the middle class from the central city to the suburban ring in our major metropolitan areas. Families that enjoy traditional high-density-neighborhood living find their housing costs rising relative to the suburban ring. This subsidy lures middle class families to low-density areas and threatens the viability of high-quality neighborhoods by reducing the number of relatively high-income households in the central city. As the number of middle-income families dwindle, the tax burden on those remaining in the problem-ridden central cities will increase. The prospect of having fewer neighbors with common inter-

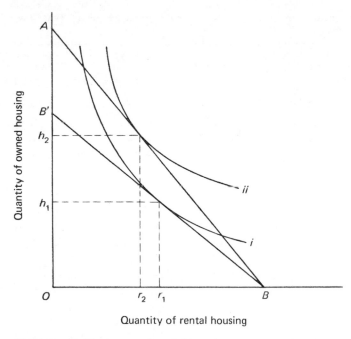

FIGURE 6.3. The impact of a subsidy to homeowners on housing consumption.

ests also tends to reduce the desirability of a residence in the central city. These added costs and declining amenities encourage higher-income groups to leave the central city and thus contribute to the decline of the urban core.

By reinforcing the decline of the central city, the downward filtering strategy has three inherent weaknesses. As already noted, such a strategy for improving the housing stock subsidizes the relatively wealthy in order to improve the well-being of low-income families. While it is not inappropriate for public policy to improve the economic well-being of middle-income groups, it should not be done under the guise of helping the poor unless this policy helps that group more effectively than any other. Secondly, by lowering the cost of suburban living relative to the central city, the downward filtering strategy undermines the neighborhoods that could easily be conserved or rehabilitated for middle class occupancy. Since rehabilitation of dwellings lowers the stock of housing available to low-income groups, there is a trade-off between the interests of the middle class and the poor. Because a program of income supplements discussed below does not foster this particular conflict of interest between income classes, this trade-off is a disadvantage of the filtering strategy.

A third weakness of this strategy for improving the housing stock is its tendency to aggravate other problems that exist in metropolitan areas. Low-density suburban developments that such policies encourage increase the automobile's dominance of the urban transportation system. This increased dependence on automobile transportation raises the levels of traffic congestion and pollution in our metropolitan areas. The downward filtering strategy also subsidizes the flight of the middle class to the suburbs in order to avoid some of the costs of upgrading the poor in central cities. To the extent urban problems are a product of this poverty, congestion, and pollution, the downward filtering strategy works against the interests of society at large.

Downward filtering of dwellings can be enhanced if the number of new units can be increased by lowering construction costs. Lower costs increase the volume of new dwellings constructed causing an increase in the number of dwellings available to low-income households. Construction costs in the past two decades have risen dramatically. From 1946 to 1968 the cost of construction rose 134 percent, compared to a rise of 64 percent for the wholesale price index for all commodities. Rising wages in the highly unionized construction trades are a major source of this increase in construction costs. The average hourly wage in construction activities rose from $1.86 in 1950 to a 1968 figure of $4.38, an increase of 135 percent.

It is often alleged that the adoption of modern industrial techniques in the construction industry would combat these rising costs and increase the volume of new construction. The reduction in costs that can be achieved by industrializing housing construction is determined by the proportion of total costs attributable to construction. The burden of taxes, utilities, and maintenance, which account for about 45 percent of monthly occupancy costs, are of course unaffected by reduced construction costs. Since industrialized housing uses the same basic material as conventional construction, costs can be reduced only by using more capital and unskilled labor in the production process.[27] Since only 10 percent of monthly occupancy costs are attributable to *on site* labor costs, a 20 percent cut in wage costs would permit only a 2 percent reduction in the final cost of housing to residents. Although the adoption of new techniques and materials may lower the cost of new construction, the impact on monthly occupancy costs will most probably be modest. The volume of new construction fostered by the reduced price is not likely to cause a significant increase in the amount of housing that filters down to poor families.

Income supplements

Giving income supplements to families unable to afford standard housing is another way, and one that is becoming increasingly popular, to improve the quality of housing. Unlike the filtering strategy, which affects supply, this approach is an attempt to increase the demand for standard housing. Because income is the primary determinant of housing expenditures, an income supplement is the logical mechanism to increase the quantity of housing services consumed by low-income households.

One form of income supplement consists of an unconditional cash grant that may be spent on any commodity. The increase in expenditures for housing caused by this type of income supplement will be determined by the income elasticity of demand for housing services. For renters, which includes most low-income households, a 1 percent change in income will cause a less than 1 percent change in housing expenditures.[28] Assuming that the income elasticity of demand for housing is .80, housing expenditures will increase .8 percent for each 1 percent increase in income. For example, consider a family whose annual income is $2,400, 25 percent of which, or $50 per month, is spent for housing. A $100 per month unconditional grant represents a 50 percent increase in income and would induce a 40 percent increase in housing expenditures, or $20 per month. A principal weakness of this approach to improving housing quality is the small portion of the grant that is likely to be used for housing.

A scheme to increase the demand for housing among low-income households could easily take the form of a guaranteed annual income. Income from this unconditional transfer payment would presumably be spent on increased consumption of necessities such as food, clothing, housing, and medical care. If the purpose of the program is to help upgrade the poor, there may be little reason to believe that increased housing expenditures will facilitate upward mobility more than, say, improved diet and medical care for children. With this view, increased housing quality is used as one of several means to facilitate upward social mobility. So long as we have limited interest in housing quality per se, the modest portion of the unconditional grant used for housing may thus be applauded rather than condemned.[29]

If the goal of public policy is to improve only the housing of low-income families, limiting subsidies to housing expenditures has a clear advantage over unconditional cash grants. Rent supplements are a method of limiting the cash grants to the purchase of housing. Assume a standard dwelling costs $X in rent per month, and the ability of a household to pay for housing is determined by its income. For example, a family may be able to spend 25 percent of its income on housing services. A subsidy or rent certificate could be issued to each household on the basis of the difference between the cost of a standard dwelling ($X) and their ability to pay. Under such a program the subsidy gets smaller as income rises, a desirable property for programs based on ability to pay.

The principal difficulty with this proposal is that a household could spend only the subsidy on housing while using its earned income for other commodities. If the subsidy is not sufficient to pay for standard housing, such households may not improve the quality of their dwelling. This problem can be avoided by requiring households to spend the amount they can pay (25 percent of their income) for a rent certificate with a face value equal to the market price for standard housing. Such a program is shown in Table 6.4, where it is assumed that a standard dwelling unit costs $75. If only $75 certificates were available, the family with no income would receive a $75 rent supplement. Families with an income of $100 per month would pay $25 for a $75 certificate if they participated in the program. Under these arrangements, a household could not legally receive a housing subsidy without purchasing a standard dwelling unit.

Both the unconditional cash grant and rent certificate programs are designed to shift the demand curve for housing to the right. Figure 6.4 shows that such programs will not only increase the quantity of housing consumed (q_2-q_1) but also result in higher prices (p_2-p_1). A major part of the subsidy may therefore be a transfer payment to the owners of low-income rental units. The proportion of the income or rent supplement that goes to owners rather than for increased housing for the poor is determined by the long-run elasticity of the housing supply. If in the long run the housing supply does not increase with a rise in the price of housing, i.e., is perfectly inelastic, all the increases in housing expenditures will be taken by landlords as increased rents. However, recent research suggests that the supply of housing is in the long run relatively elastic.[30] If this is correct, property owners would reap benefits from the programs through higher prices only in the short run. In

TABLE 6.4 A hypothetical rent supplement scheme when standard housing costs $75 per month

Household monthly income	Ability to pay	Subsidy
$000	$000	$75
100	25	50
200	50	25
300	75	0

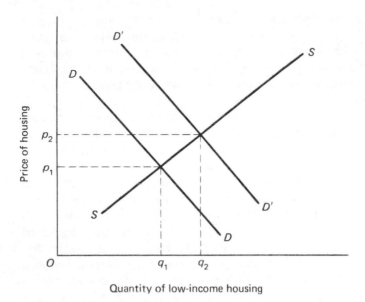

FIGURE 6.4. The impact of an increase in demand on the low-
income housing market.

the long run, the program of income supplements would aid the low-
income households for which it was designed.

TOWARD AN URBAN HOUSING POLICY

Two basic tenets should provide the basis for a successful housing
policy. One is that housing policy should facilitate the integration of
low-income households into the mainstream of American socioeconomic life. Housing is only one aspect of antipoverty policy, and programs to house the poor must be coordinated with other attempts to
upgrade the poor. By narrowly specifying good housing as a standard
dwelling unit, many public housing projects have provided a monoto-
nous as well as an unsafe, institutionalized environment that increases
the resident's sense of alienation from society. Using resources to guarantee this kind of publicly provided standard housing for the poor may
frustrate the upgrading of the low socioeconomic strata of the society.
These housing expenditures undermine the upgrading of the poor by
taking resources away from more productive antipoverty programs. For
example, a fixed number of dollars might be better spent on educating
the poor rather than on their housing. In this context it makes little sense

to allocate resources to housing the poor if the same financial effort applied to some other antipoverty program would better facilitate their upward mobility. If poverty were eliminated, households might choose substandard housing but would not have it thrust upon them. A successful antipoverty program will reduce the need for a housing policy designed to improve the living conditions of the poor.

A neglected aspect of housing policy is the provision of effective consumer choice among different residential life styles for the middle class. Traditional city neighborhood living is an option most easily maintained by the rehabilitation and conservation of older portions of our metropolitan areas. When renewing decayed areas of the central city, care must be taken not to homogenize residential patterns. Effective consumer choice requires viable areas of high-rise apartment buildings, high-density but low-rise single and multifamily unit neighborhoods as well as the land-intensive suburban style of living. A housing program that does not preserve and foster these alternatives is a policy that denies the city one of its basic purposes: economies of scale in consumption.

NOTES

[1] Public Law 171, 81st Congress, S 1070.

[2] "A Theory of Human Motivation," *Psychological Reviews* 50 (May 1943): 370–398. Physiological needs (food, sex) are lowest in the hierarchy followed by safety and security, affection, esteem, self-actualization, cognition, and aesthetic experience.

[3] Alvin L. Schorr, "Housing and Its Effect," in H. M. Proshansky, et. al., eds., *Environmental Psychology* (New York: Holt, Rinehart & Winston, 1967), p. 320.

[4] Jane Jacobs, *The Death and Life of Great American Cities* (New York: Random House, 1961).

[5] E. L. Ryan, "Personal Identity in an Urban Slum," in Leonard J. Duhl, ed., *The Urban Condition* (New York: Basic Books, 1963), ch. 11.

[6] William H. Michelson, *Man and His Urban Environment: A Sociological Approach* (Reading, Mass.: Addison-Wesley, 1970), p. 68.

[7] M. Fried and P. Gleicher, "Residential Satisfaction in an Urban Slum," *Journal of the American Institute of Planners* 27 (November 1961): 305–315.

[8] M. Fried, "Grieving for a Lost Home," in Leonard J. Duhl, ed., op. cit., ch. 12.

[9] Jane Jacobs, op. cit., pp. 81–82.

[10] For a summary of this literature, see William H. Michelson, op. cit., ch. 3.

[11] Comparisons of housing quality over time are complicated by the changing definition. In 1950, dilapidated dwellings with or without plumbing facilities were classified as substandard. Inadequate initial construction, such as dirt floors or makeshift walls, is one criterion for dilapidation. Alternatively, dilapidated dwellings have major deficiencies, such as sagging walls, or a combination of minor deficiencies that make the dwelling unsafe or inadequate shelter. Data on dilapidation, however, is unavailable in the 1970 *Census of Housing*, and substandard dwellings are those without all plumbing facilities. These are, of course, very crude measures of housing quality, since a rat-infested slum in 1970 could appear as a "standard" dwelling unit. The statistics in the text use the 1970 definition of housing quality based on the availability of plumbing facilities.

[12] For an analysis of government farm subsidies and their effect on food prices, see Paul A. Samuelson, *Economics*, 7th ed. (New York: McGraw-Hill, 1967), pp. 397–404.

[13] In game theory the Prisoner's Dilemma is described as follows: "Two suspects are taken into custody and separated. The district attorney is certain they are guilty of a specific crime, but he does not have adequate evidence to convict them at a trial. He points out to each prisoner that each has two alternatives: to confess to the crime the police are sure they have done, or not to confess. If they both do not confess, then the district attorney states he will book them on some very minor trumped-up charge such as petty larceny and illegal possession of a weapon, and they will both receive minor punishment; if they both confess, they will be prosecuted, but he will recommend less than the most severe sentence; but if one confesses and the other does not, then the confessor will receive lenient treatment for turning state's evidence whereas the latter will get 'the book' slapped at him." The dilemma is that without collusion, the rational choice for each is to confess. R. Duncan Luce and Howard Raiffa, *Games and Decisions* (New York: Wiley, 1957), p. 95. See also, Otto A. Davis and Andrew B. Whinston, "The Economics of Urban Renewal," in James Q. Wilson, ed., *Urban Renewal: The Record and The Controversy* (Cambridge: M.I.T. Press, 1966), ch. 3.

[14] If both owners can receive a higher rate of return on some other investment, they are not likely to improve their property. The Prisoner's Dilemma shows that interdependencies may lower the expected rate of return on property improvements. It does not suggest that there are not better investment opportunities elsewhere in the economy, even when the best possible return on property improvements is guaranteed.

[15] Jacobs, op. cit., p. 11.

[16] *Hearings Before the National Commission on Urban Problems* (Washington, D.C.: Government Printing Office, 1968), vol. 1, p. 256.

[17] Dick Netzer, *Economics of the Property Tax* (Washington, D.C.: The Brookings Institution, 1966), p. 166.

[18] This inherent weakness in the property tax can be circumvented by the land tax proposed by Henry George in his *Progress and Poverty* (1880). By taxing only the value of land, the land tax removes the disincentive to invest in buildings inherent in current methods of taxation. The advantages of the land tax are analyzed in greater detail in Chapter 8.

[19] Martin Anderson has described urban renewal as a bulldozer that destroys more housing than

it creates. See Anderson, *The Federal Bulldozer* (Cambridge: M.I.T. Press, 1964). For criticisms of this interpretation of urban renewal, see James Q. Wilson, ed., ap., Part VII.

[20] Edgar O. Olsen, "A Competitive Theory of the Housing Market," *American Economic Review* 59 (September 1969): p. 619.

[21] This position is verified in Chester Hartman, "The Housing of Relocated Families," *Journal of the American Institute of Planners*, vol. 30, no. 4 (November 1964): 266–286. Reprinted in James Q. Wilson, ed., op. cit., ch. 10.

[22] Basil Zimmer, "The Small Businessman and Relocation," in James Q. Wilson, ed., op. cit., ch. 14.

[23] *Hearings Before National Commission,* vol. 1, p. 199.

[24] Martin J. Bailey has made a case for renewal with a model based on residential discrimination against minority groups. "A Note on the Economics of Residential Zoning and Urban Renewal," *Land Economics* 35 (August 1959): 288–292.

[25] The ownership of individual units within multifamily dwellings is becoming increasingly popular. These condominiums are a relatively recent development that could greatly facilitate the survival of the central city in the long run. Of course, the interest deductions have primarily subsidized the construction of single family dwellings units.

[26] Owners of multifamily dwellings have also been subsidized through laws such as those that allow accelerated depreciation, a practice that greatly increases the profitability of these investments. Increased profitability encourages more construction and, ceteris paribus, a decline in the market price of an apartment. Subsidizing the wealthy in this case filters benefits to families of more modest means. Although both owned and nonowned housing have been subsidized to some extent, the bias remains in favor of home ownership because the subsidy rises with family income.

[27] Mobile homes are a type of industrialized housing that is inexpensive, partly because they are constructed with cheaper materials. The relatively short-term financing (10 years) that is typically available for their purchase testifies to the inferior quality of their construction. By contrast, 30-year financing is available for most conventional homes. These credit restrictions greatly increase the monthly occupancy costs to residents of mobile homes.

[28] Frank de Leeuw, "The Demand for Housing: A Review of Cross Section Evidence," in *Review of Economics and Statistics* 53 (February 1971): 1–11. De Leeuw estimates the income elasticity of demand for rental housing (% ΔQ/% ΔY) to be .80.

[29] Milton Friedman argues for unconditional grants on the grounds that households know their needs better than an agency of the government. For his nineteenth-century liberal position, the issue is one of paternalism that undermines the individual's control over his environment. The position stated here is different from Friedman's in that it recognizes the unconditional grant as a way of manipulating the individual in society. There is no intellectual commitment to unconditional grants. Thus if better housing were crucial to socioeconomic advance, limiting the grants to the purchase of housing would be acceptable. The essential difference between the two positions lies in the specification of the desired end. For Friedman, public action should maximize utility as perceived by the recipients, while the alternative is to maximize the welfare of the donors (taxpayers), who presumably have some benevolent reasons for their action. There are, of course, difficult problems associated with each view. See Milton Friedman, *Capitalism and Freedom* (Chicago: University of Chicago Press, 1962).

[30] R. F. Muth, "The Demand for Non-Farm Housing," in A. C. Harberger, ed., *The Demand for Durable Goods* (Chicago: University of Chicago Press, 1960), p. 58.

RECOMMENDED READING

Fried, Marc and Peggy Gleicher, "Some Sources of Satisfaction in an Urban Slum," *Journal of the American Institute of Planners* 27 (November 1961): 305–315. Reprinted in D. W. Rasmussen and C. T. Haworth, eds., *The Modern City: A Book of Readings.* New York: Harper & Row, 1973.

Gans, Herbert J. "The Failure of Urban Renewal," *Commentary,* April 1955. Reprinted in Rasmussen and Haworth, op. cit.

Jacobs, Jane. *The Death and Life of Great American Cities.* New York: Random House, 1961.

Michelson, William M. *Man and His Urban Environment: A Sociological Approach.* Reading, Mass.: Addison-Wesley, 1970.

Olsen, Edgar O. "A Competitive Theory of the Housing Market." *American Economic Review* 59 (September 1969). Reprinted in Rasmussen and Haworth, op. cit.

Wilson, James Q., ed. *Urban Renewal: The Record and the Controversy.* Cambridge: M.I.T. Press, 1966.

7
THE URBAN
TRANSPORTATION SYSTEM

The purpose of concentrating large populations in urban areas is to increase the number of contacts among people. These contacts may be for the purpose of facilitating production, increasing economies of scale in consumption, and/or improving the socioeconomic status of the population. Individual units within an urban area are tied into a vast web of communication by the urban transportation system. The advantages of urban living would be neutralized without the communication and exchange provided by an effective transportation network. Mobility within urban areas is thus an important component in the smooth operation of the urban economy.

Effective communication has generally required that people or things be moved into positions of proximity. Dealings between business firms require the movement of inputs and outputs; traditionally, people could communicate only through face-to-face contact. Need for physical proximity of people has been reduced by the telephone, which permits instantaneous communication over long distances. The importance of mobility in communication is reduced by modern technology. August Heckscher has argued that modern work "requires the processing of information, and the intangible can be so instantaneously and so cheaply flashed across space that it must seem absurd to move cumbrous human bodies."[1] Urban transportation problems are the result of past technologies, which required physical movement in order to communicate. If future technological advances permit communication through electronic means, which lower the need for mobility within metropolitan areas, the urban transportation problem will be greatly reduced. In the extreme, such technological advance could eliminate the city as we now know it. There is, of course, no guarantee that the problems solved by such a technological demise of cities would not be replaced by even more troublesome social afflictions. It is assumed in this chapter that technological advance in the foreseeable future will not greatly reduce the need or desirability of geographic mobility within our metropolitan areas.

High-quality transportation services are not only important for the functioning of the urban economy; they are also a commodity used by consumers. Much time, energy, and income are spent by people moving within urban areas, since transportation accounts for about 10 percent of all outlays for consumption by urban families. Automobile congestion and poor quality public transit services increase the monetary and psychic costs of urban mobility, thereby lowering the welfare of the population. In lowering the costs of urban mobility, an effective transportation policy improves the welfare of area residents directly by lowering the costs associated with a major item in the typical consumer's budget, and indirectly by improving communication among socioeconomic units in the city.

THE TRANSPORTATION CRISIS: REAL OR IMAGINED?

The crisis in the urban transportation system, like the urban crisis in general, is a much disputed phenomenon. There are many apostles of the viewpoint that sees a transportation monster about to seal the fate of our urban areas. Tabor R. Stone argues that the transportation problems generated by the automobile pose a threat to society—a threat that has full support from a masochistic public:

> We are facing a transportation crisis, one that becomes more critical as time goes on, a crisis which threatens to overwhelm us . . . we are neglecting (in terms of planner based control) a transportation system that has been built up by industry, certain governmental agencies and an enthusiastic public . . . that is undeniably a dominant factor in the urban environment.[2]

A less threatening diagnosis based on the negative externalities generated by the transportation system is offered by Ezra J. Mishan:

> ". . . it is impossible not to dwell for a moment on the most notorious by-product of industrialization the world has ever known: the appalling traffic congestion in our towns, cities and suburbs. One consequence is that the pleasures of strolling along the streets of a city are more of a memory than a current pastime. Lorries, motorcycles and taxis belching fumes, filth and stench, snarling engines and unabating visual disturbance have compounded to make movement through the city an ordeal for the

pedestrian at the same time as the mutual strangulation of the traffic makes it a purgatory for motorists."[3]

Responsibility of private automobile transportation for this crisis is made explicit: "No major city in the country has escaped automobile poisoning . . . all display the same symptoms of debilitation; all have been weakened by the same dehumanizing fever."[4] Shortcomings of the urban transportation system are underscored by the 50,000 people killed annually on America's highways.

An alternative view is based on the proposition that the urban transportation crisis is more imagined than real. John R. Meyer claims this crisis is a product of exaggerated expectations regarding the improvements increased transportation facilities would bring:

> . . . in our modern affluent society an improvement from 25 to 30 or 35 miles an hour or so in the average performance speed of private transportation systems during the rush hours has not satisfied some commuters. This is particularly true since many of them have chosen to give up the improved time by living further away from their work places.[5]

Estimates of time spent during the typical work trip in six major metropolitan areas is less than 16 minutes, Philadelphia having the longest average work trip of 20.1 minutes.[6] If the average work trip is made during the peak load hours, these times reflect the performance of the transportation system at its worst. Since it appears that most workers do not spend excessive amounts of time in travel from home to job, the transportation crisis may be more imagined than real.

Debate on the existence of an urban transportation crisis reflects a general uncertainty as to the nature of the urban transportation problem. Oi and Shuldiner express their doubt: "Is it traffic congestion, inadequate parking facilities, suburban sprawl or declining transit services and patronage?"[7] Such transportation phenomena as automobile congestion and declining transit services frequently stir an emotional reaction that yields a crisis analysis generating more heat than light. A principal obstacle to defining the urban transportation problem and improving analysis of it is the inability to specify the purpose or goals of the transit system. The confusion lies "in the inability to specify an objective function for urban transportation. Is low cost transportation the goal, or is the minimization of commuter time? To what extent are commuters' wishes to be respected? . . . Is traffic safety an objective function or a constraint. . . ."[8]

Without a clear notion of the purpose of the urban transportation system, it is impossible to identify either successful operation or failure of crisis proportion. As a component of the larger urban system, the transportation network can be analyzed from its role in facilitating the smooth operation of the urban area. Purposes of the urban transportation system are thus derived from that of the city itself: the realization of externalities in production, providing economies of scale in consumption, and facilitating the upgrading function.

THE ISSUES

Broad objectives of the urban transportation network must be consistent with the purposes of the city itself. Charles Zwick offered such a view when he wrote, "The ultimate goal is to improve urban living, not to eliminate congestion, or maintain investments in real estate or transportation facilities as such."[9] Policy issues are clarified when the urban transportation system is analyzed as one component of a complex metropolitan economy; such an approach helps define the role of the transportation network within the larger system.

Facilitating externalities in production is a function of the city that is accomplished by communication between business firms. A major part of this interaction is performed by the transportation network, which delivers materials and business services to the firm. If the metropolitan area is to facilitate externalities in production, the smooth flow of goods and services is required. In the modern city this movement is accomplished through the use of motorized vehicles; congestion of roads interrupts this flow of commodities and raises the costs of transporting goods and services between business firms. Traffic congestion is an issue that transportation policy must face, since it may frustrate a basic function of urban agglomeration—fostering externalities in production.

This problem is particularly bothersome in areas such as the traditional high-density central city, the origin or destination of many trips. Although it was argued in Chapter 5 that the high-density central city is a viable location for many business firms, congestion can threaten its existence by raising the cost of production to firms in the central business district. Labor costs rise because the longer trip to work means that many employees must be compensated for the extra time in transit inasmuch as their real income is reduced. Similarly, there is a rise in transportation costs associated with the delivery of raw materials and final products. Congestion of the high-density central city can pose a threat to the viability of business firms in that part of the metropolitan area.[10]

It was argued in the previous chapter that the continued existence of the high-density central city offers residents an alternative life style and a larger market basket of goods and service from which to choose.

If congestion were to undermine the viability of a central city location for most business firms, this economy of scale in consumption offered by large metropolitan areas would be eliminated. From the consumer's viewpoint, congestion also raises the monetary and psychic costs of intraurban travel. Effective operation of cities requires that transportation policy combat congestion because it frustrates two purposes of urban agglomeration.

A high-density central city makes effective mass transportation possible because many people must travel along similar routes. The existence of public transportation to a high-density central city can improve the well-being of consumers in three ways: (1) by increasing the mobility of nondrivers; (2) by reducing the need to own one or more than one automobile; and (3) by relieving some of the congestion caused by automobiles.

An alternative to private automobile transportation clearly enhances the mobility of the young, the elderly, and members of impoverished households who do not have access to an automobile. The poor are the most likely persons to be rendered immobile since they can least afford taxis, a major form of public transit in a transportation system dominated by the automobile. Since households in poverty generally cannot afford to purchase an automobile, public transportation facilities increase their mobility. Second, a viable mass-transit system increases consumer welfare by reducing the need of households to own more than one vehicle. If the work trip can be made from the suburban ring to the central city via public transit, the household is less likely to require more than one automobile. Aside from the increase in utility because the worker is not forced to drive to work, consumer welfare rises because required expenditures for automobile transportation are reduced. By reducing the necessity of multiple car ownership, the real income of households is increased because they have fewer required expenditures. Finally, consumers are better off because a mass transit system reduces the number of cars on the highway, making automobile trips quicker, safer, and more pleasant.

The urban transportation system can also influence the effectiveness of the urban upgrading function. As noted in Chapter 3, poor households that do not own an automobile are isolated from the increasing proportion of jobs located in the suburban fringe of our metropolitan areas. If the transportation system could be altered to improve the accessibility of jobs to these households, their climb up the socioeconomic ladder might be speeded. Independent of its influence on the mobility of the poor, transportation policy has frequently worked against the interests of low-income households. The annals of transportation planning tell of many expressways built through large concentrations of low-quality housing. These roads lower the cost of intraurban mobility to automobile owners while raising the cost of housing to the poor because the supply of low-cost dwellings is reduced. In earlier years the elimination of slums was considered a benefit of expressway development because planners perceived the problem to be the existence of blight, not the low income of the residents. As one element in a broader urban system, transportation policy should not counteract efforts to improve the socioeconomic status of the poor.

There are three issues that constitute the urban transportation problem. Because congestion raises the costs of the communication that is a principal advantage of urban life, its regulation is an important function of government. Secondly, the transportation system should facilitate consumer choice among alternative modes of travel and should support residential areas of high density. It should not work to homogenize the metropolitan region. Finally, meeting the transportation needs of the poor should be an integral part of public policy.

Recent discussions of transportation policy have often focused on the pollution emitted from the private automobile that dominates urban travel patterns. The automobile is undeniably a major contributor to the fouling of the atmosphere, and in many areas it is the principal source of air pollution. The percentage of all air pollution resulting from the use of the internal combustion engine varies considerably between regions, but the generally accepted average for urban areas is 60 percent.[11] Denis Hayes describes pollution in Los Angeles more dramatically:

> Fumes from automobile exhaust pipes have turned the skies above the city a weird shade of yellowish green. . . . On many days of every year the accumulated smog is so unbearable that school children are not allowed to play outdoors. Last year someone placed a hand-lettered sign at the city limits: BREATHING IS UNHEALTHY FOR CHILDREN AND OTHER GROWING THINGS.[12]

If pollution of the atmosphere has reached the critical proportions that many ecologists claim, control of this negative externality generated by the transportation system is imperative.

When debating the relative merits of the private automobile and various types of public transportation, however, the issue of air pollution *should not* be relevant. Health hazards created by automobile exhausts are not a consequence of that mode of transportation but rather result from our unwillingness to *control* the technological characteristics of private passenger vehicles. Available technology in a society that can place a man on the moon would permit the production of a virtually pollution-free car. An increase in public transit expenditures *because the present automobile pollutes the environment* would be based on a distortion of the realities of urban transportation. The policy choice between modes of transportation should be made on the desirability of a *pollution-free car* relative to other modes of transit. Producing the pollution-free car is not an urban problem but rather a question of industrial organization and the nature of controls over the production of goods and services in a modern industrial society.[13] Unfortunately, private business firms in America generally have an excessively large influence over production decisions that affect the entire society. Pollution of the environment provides a dramatic case in point.

AUTOMOBILES: THE PEOPLE'S CHOICE

Modern American cities are characterized by a transportation system dominated by the private automobile. As shown in Table 7.1, the total number of passengers carried by three major modes of mass transit fell from 17.1 billion in 1950 to a 1967 figure of 8.2 billion, a decline of 52 percent. Reduced patronage of public transportation is a logical consequence of the suburbanization of economic activity and the rise in automobile ownership. A dramatic increase in the number of multicar families is shown in Table 7.2. Forces responsible for the popularity of automobile transportation must be investigated before we turn to the optimum mix of public transit and automobile use within the transportation system.

Individuals generally choose between public and private modes of transportation. Public transportation is either "personalized" service, such as that offered by taxicabs, or is bus or rail mass transit, while automobiles dominate the private transportation system. The process by which individuals choose between public and private means of transportation must be analyzed as two separate choices. An individual must first choose a basic means of travel, i.e., will he rely on public transit or will he purchase an automobile. Once the decision to purchase an

TABLE 7.1 Passengers carried by public and private transit companies, 1950–1967 (in millions)

Type of transit	1950	1967	Percentage change
Electric railway cars	6,168	2,201	−64
Trolley coaches	1,658	248	−85
Motor buses	9,420	5,723	−39
Total	17,146	8,172	−52

SOURCE: U.S. Bureau of the Census, *Statistical Abstract of the United States, 1969* (Washington, D.C.: Government Printing Office, 1969), p. 554.

TABLE 7.2 Family automobile ownership, 1950–1968

Families owning	1950 (percent)	1968 (percent)	Percentage change
One automobile	52	53	+ 2
Two or more	7	26	+271
One or more	59	79	+ 34

SOURCE: U.S. Bureau of the Census, *Statistical Abstract of the United States, 1969* (Washington, D.C.: Government Printing Office, 1969), p. 552.

automobile is made, a complete model of travel patterns must be able to explain why many auto owners periodically ride public transportation. The process of individual mode choice is analyzed in this section.

When deciding whether or not to purchase an automobile, an individual unencumbered by past decisions weighs the costs and benefits associated with the various modes of transportation. Since the relationship between transportation cost and number of trips varies between modes, the number of trips a consumer expects to take will influence his choice of transportation. In particular, the advantages of automobile ownership increase with the number of trips a consumer expects to make.

Changes in the total cost of transportation as the number of trips is varied is shown in Figure 7.1 for both public transit and the private automobile. Solid line segment *OA* shows the total money cost resulting from any number of trips on public transportation. Because there is no cost on public transit if no trips are taken, the cost function is a ray through the origin. It is a straight line because the consumer of public transit faces an unchanging market price for the transportation service. The average cost of a ride on public transit is therefore the same as an additional ride, i.e., average cost equals marginal cost. The slope of *OA* is the marginal cost per ride of public transportation while total cost is the product of the number of rides and the price per trip.

Because of the fixed costs associated with the purchase of the car, the relationship between cost and expected number of trips for automobile owners differs from that of public transport patrons. In addition to the purchase price of the car, there are insurance, license, and some maintenance costs unrelated to the number of trips taken. In Figure 7.1, distance *OB* reflects these fixed costs to the automobile owner. Segment *BC* shows the relationship between the expected number of trips and total money cost; it also shows the marginal cost of a trip by private automobile to be less than that of a trip by public transit. This occurs because the public transit system is likely to adopt average cost pricing in order to recover the costs of the fixed investment. Hence

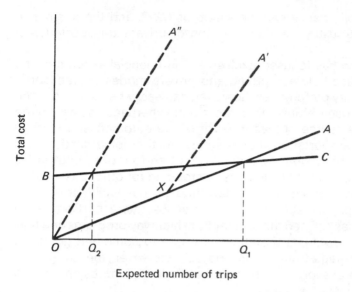

FIGURE 7.1. The relationship between total cost and expected
number of trips for public and private transit.

the marginal cost to the consumer of an additional trip on public transit
will include some payment on the fixed capital costs of the system.
Since the owner of the automobile must pay the entire fixed cost of
the automobile regardless of whether he takes any trips at all, the
change in total cost with respect to an additional trip (marginal cost)
is merely gasoline, oil, parking, and depreciation due to the trip.

Faced with these money cost functions, the expected number of trips
will be a major factor in determining whether the consumer will rely
on public or private transportation. If he expects to take fewer than
OQ_1 trips, public transit (segment OA) will provide the less expensive
service. On the other hand, the automobile is preferred from this func-
tional point of view if the number of trips is expected to exceed OQ_1.
The cost function (OA) implies that the consumer uses only one form
of public transportation, since taxicabs are more expensive than buses
or rail transit. A high-density transportation corridor makes many destinations accessible via public transit. Trips along the mass transit routes
will cost less than those to destinations that are located in less dense
areas that can be reached only via individualized public transit, i.e., a
taxicab. In such a situation, consumers are likely to face a kinked cost
function for public transportation. The primary trips associated with
work and shopping within the high-density area would be cheaper than
those to areas of urban sprawl. Under these circumstances, the cost

function for public transit has the shape of *OXA'*, and the number of trips required to justify the consumption of private transportation is reduced.

This discussion has focused exclusively on financial aspects of the consumer's choice between public and private modes of transportation. Nonpecuniary preferences, however, can easily be included in the analysis. It has been argued that the frontier heritage in the United States may be a source of bias in favor of the automobile, a form of individualized transportation that is similar to the horse used on the frontier. With either mode the individual is free to move about at his whim, with no concern for schedules or stopping for other passengers. This anticollectivist strain in American thought may well increase the appeal of the private automobile. Former Secretary of Commerce Luther Hodges has claimed that cutbacks in highway programs and tolls that reduce traffic volume threaten "our right to come and go as we please . . . a heritage from frontier days."[14] However, the preference for automobile transportation in most developed countries appears to weaken this "cultural" argument.

The private automobile is also a "luxury" form of travel in that it provides comfort, audio entertainment, and privacy at a relatively low price. Moskowitz explained these advantages in detail:

> I live in the suburbs, 8.8 miles from where I work. It costs me $317 a year, or 26.50 per month, to commute. . . . I set my time for going and coming. I have a comfortable seat and privacy. I keep dry in rainy weather, and it takes 24 minutes from my door to the door of the office. . . . If I cared to give up the flexibility of schedule and about 5 more minutes, I could join with two fellow workers, ride in a newer car, and cut my costs by about two thirds.[15]

Demand for comfort and convenience appears to be unaffected by price, i.e., is relatively price inelastic. Moses and Williamson found that a reduction of the bus fare to zero in Cook County, Illinois, would cause only a 13 percent decline in the use of the automobile.[16] If consumers dislike public transportation for nonpecuniary reasons, in effect they view the average cost of mass transit to be the dotted line *OA"* in Figure 7.1. These preferences will reduce from OQ_1 to OQ_2 the number of trips required to purchase an automobile.

Any forces tending to increase the number of trips taken by an individual will encourage the use of the private automobile as a mode of transportation. Rising prices and reduced service of most metropolitan public transportation systems unwittingly reinforce the trend toward automobile use. Inadequate service encourages some riders to switch entirely to the private automobile. Reduced patronage lowers revenue and encourages further cutbacks of service, beginning a vicious cycle that culminates in the demise of the public transportation system.

An automobile owner is unlikely to patronize the public transportation system under normal circumstances. This can be shown by the relationship between total variable cost and the number of trips taken. Total variable cost is merely total cost minus fixed cost. Hence in Figure 7.2, *OBC* is derived from segment *BC* in Figure 7.1, while *OA* remains unchanged. The fact that the ray *OBC* is everywhere below *OA* suggests that an automobile owner would never ride public transit because the marginal cost of an additional trip on the latter mode is higher. We do observe, however, that automobile owners sometimes do ride public transit, suggesting that the bias in favor of private transportation may not threaten the long-run viability of public modes of travel.

There are two factors that tend to undermine the dominance of private transportation in metropolitan areas. Work trips are usually taken at a time of peak load demand for transportation services, a phenomenon that creates congestion on the highway. This congestion tends to raise the cost of private auto transit for a trip that has a very small luxury component. If the lowest time- and money-consuming mode is demanded for the work trip, and congestion raises the cost of private transportation beyond *OA* (say to *OD*) in Figure 7.2, the consumer will be attracted to public transit. It must be noted, however, that the performance of bus transit is also impaired by congestion, suggest-

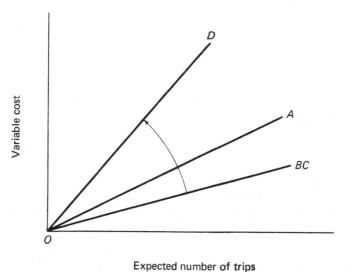

FIGURE 7.2. The relationship between variable cost and expected number of trips for public and private transit.

ing that this form is not a suitable alternative unless buses are given special status on the highways during the times of congestion.

A second factor encouraging the use of public transit for the work trip is the opportunity cost of using the private mode when the number of drivers exceeds the number of automobiles belonging to the household. Trips to work usually involve a single destination, while those made by housewives often include many stops for shopping and child care. When it is available, households have the option of using public transit for the work trip rather than purchasing a second car or leaving nonworkers without transportation. Because they have many other needs, most families can ill afford the cost of a second vehicle. Since only 26 percent of all households owned two or more cars in 1968, an alternative to the private automobile significantly increases consumer welfare by lowering the cost of transportation. However, this factor may become less important as per capita income rises, because U.S. families appear to have a high income elasticity of demand for a second car.

An affluent society is likely to have a significant bias in favor of the automobile over public transportation for its primary source of geographic mobility. Although congestion is likely to undermine this bias in the long run, it is liable to encourage the use of public transit for the work trip but not for other trips with a "luxury" element. Implications for the urban economy of the bias towards the automobile is the subject of the rest of this chapter.

TRANSPORTATION POLICY

Individual preferences for private automobile transportation are apt to foster a transportation system that, from the social point of view, is inefficient. If private decisions affect other people adversely, society may need to intervene in order to minimize these undesired externalities. Congestion is a social cost because each driver imposes a cost on other highway users. A transportation system dominated by the private automobile also raises the cost of transportation in high-density central cities, undermining their viability and reducing the range of choices available to consumers. The impact of congestion on consumer welfare and methods of combating it are analyzed in this section.

Congestion as a social cost

A divergence between private and social costs associated with congestion is easily demonstrated.[17] Assume there is one route between two points with a normal downward sloping demand curve for the use of this route. As shown by demand curve *DD* in Figure 7.3, a decline in the "price" (including variable costs of the automobile, time, and tolls) of road usage will encourage more vehicles to use the facility. The cost of an automobile trip along the route is constant at *OA* until the point at which additional traffic creates congestion. Additional motorists must now pay a higher price for the same road trip because of the increased time required for the journey. This is shown by the cost curve *AA*, which includes out-of-pocket costs and time. Motorists will continue to enter the highway until the cost of the journey exceeds the price they are willing and able to pay. Given the cost and demand curves in Figure 7.3, the equilibrium number of vehicles on the highway will be *OC*. The entry of vehicles causing congestion (*BC*) raises the cost of the trip to the original *OB* vehicles by the amount of the shaded area (*EAFG*). Because the additional motorists consider only private costs and not the added burden to other drivers, social costs exceed private costs.[18] The added social cost of an additional vehicle exceeds the price paid by that motorist, and a reduction in the number of vehicles on the highway from *OC* would increase aggregate well-being.

Pricing congestion away

In the short run, congestion is generally treated by economists as a so-called peak-load pricing problem. When highway capacity is fixed,

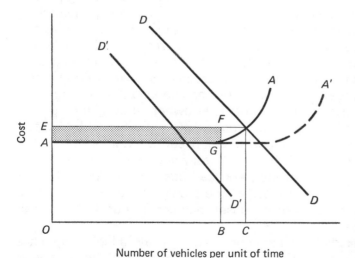

FIGURE 7.3. The social cost of automobile congestion and alternatives for public policy.

the excess demand for its use indicates that the price of travel at the peak load hours is too low. If the number of vehicles using a highway falls when price increases, a system of tolls would eliminate congestion. A toll for automobile use on congested highways would discourage nonessential trips and encourage the use of various modes of public transportation. One method of implementing such a system would be to construct toll booths, to be manned during the rush hours, on major expressways heading into the central city. In order to encourage maximum use of automobile capacity, the size of the toll could be based on the difference between vehicle carrying capacity and the actual number of passengers. If the toll is 50 cents per "missing" passenger, a six-passenger car carrying only three people would pay $1.50. A full car would pay no toll. Such a scheme would encourage commuters either to use automobile capacity more effectively or to use public transportation.

Unfortunately, stopping to pay a toll slows the flow of traffic, thus aggravating the very congestion that caused the construction of toll booths. An alternative method of collecting tolls is to place in each car an electronic identifier that registers all entries into the congested areas, for which the user would be billed each month.[19] Such technological solutions to the congestion problem require large initial outlays for electronic equipment and the development of a substantial bureaucracy to collect the revenue.

A simpler method of raising the cost of highway use during peak hours would be to increase central city parking fees. Making parking expensive for the work day (8 A.M. to 5 P.M.) and offering free parking facilities near suburban rapid-transit terminals would induce workers to ride public transportation.[20] Workers who use an automobile on the job, such as salesmen, would be unaffected by the peak load price because they do not park for long periods of time. Similarly, downtown shoppers could be encouraged by low-cost short-term parking. An inequity inherent in this approach is that automobile owners driving through the central city contribute to congestion but are not affected by the toll. This may not be a singificant drawback because automobile trips terminating in the central city are most easily and comfortably made by public transportation. Perhaps peak load costs should be higher for these auto drivers than for those whose trip is more difficult on public transportation owing to an increased number of transfers that can cause trip delays.

Charging peak load users of congested highways a higher price has an effect on the income distribution. A peak price favors the rich, who are willing to spend money to avoid the loss of time, while the required increase in dollar outlays will reduce the welfare of poor persons, who often have more time than money. This regressive aspect of a peak load price is compounded since it is easier for upper-income groups to avoid the congestion levy—they often have more flexibility in their work schedules than do workers with less skill. The impact of a peak-load pricing policy on the income distribution is easily illustrated. Consider the impact of a 50-cent peak load price on two families, each of whose head-of-household works in the central city but lives in the suburban ring. One earns $20,000 per year and the other $5,000. Working every day for 50 weeks requires a total of $250 per year in peak load prices to combat congestion. Assuming (heroically) that a poverty budget of $3,700 will cover necessities for each family, the peak load price will take away less than 2 percent of the wealthy family's "discretionary" budget. The lower-income family, on the other hand, must pay 19 percent of its resources not required for necessities. It has been argued that "time prices differ from money prices, however, since they appear relatively lower to persons with a lower money value of time . . . a congestion charge in money is likely to be regressive in its effects."[21] Viewing time as cost suggests there is no short-run congestion problem because the increased time of travel imposes an optimal peak-load price. All users reveal their willingness to spend the time, i.e., pay the price. Since a money peak-load price discriminates against the poor while a time price has the opposite bias, it is not clear which is the better policy.

Unclogging highways with highways

This dilemma associated with peak load pricing can be avoided in the long run by reducing the level of congestion. One method is to increase the number of automobiles the transportation system can handle; this would, in effect, shift the cost curve in Figure 7.3 from AA to AA'. Although it has widespread support, there are two arguments against the expansion of highway capacity to relieve burdens imposed by congestion.

If roadways are expanded, they may eventually require so much land that the central city is destroyed—and with it the need for more highway capacity. Expropriating land from commercial, residential, and governmental uses for roads and parking may create a situation where people find the central city very accessible but are without a reason for going there. A more immediate threat to the vitality of the central city is the loss of city tax revenues that accompanies the taking of land from the private sector for use as public highways. Highway expansion will continue to be self-defeating as long as municipal governments receive most of their revenues from property taxes and as long as inadequate public services undermine the central city. Expanding highway capacity may be an inappropriate way to combat congestion because it will eventually be too expensive in terms of the land required to solve the problem.

Moskowitz has answered this criticism by arguing that the land-intensive nature of the highway solution is exaggerated. He shows that in 1960 Los Angeles freeways occupied only 1.6 percent of the total land area.[22] Since one projection places the freeway needs of 1980 Los Angeles at four times the 1960 level, Moskowitz's estimate suggests that the proportion of total land taken up by freeways alone in that year will be 6.4 percent.[23] Increased traffic flows will require expansion of other streets and off-street parking, raising the proportion of land area that must be devoted to the highway network. Increasing population in our large urban areas suggests that automobile-oriented solutions to the congestion problem are likely to be suboptimal because of the large amounts of land devoured by highways.

Even if highways will not consume too much land in the immediate future, increased capacity may not reduce congestion during hours of peak demand. Better performance after the construction of new highway capacity makes the automobile a more attractive mode of travel relative to public transit alternatives. A new, uncongested highway will attract additional drivers because the relative price of automobile travel is reduced, resulting in an increase in demand that will again cause overcrowding.[24] Lowering the cost of automobile travel within metropolitan areas reinforces the bias towards the automobile. A policy of expanding highway capacity to reduce congestion is likely to offer relief only in the short run and possibly at the price of the destruction of the high-density central city.

Reducing the peak load demand for highways

An alternative way to combat congestion is to reduce the demand for automobile travel during peak load hours. Shifting the demand curve to $D'D'$ in Figure 7.3 would permit the free flow of traffic on the highway. In some cases, a staggering of the work day could reduce the level of congestion by spreading the peak load volume over a longer period of time. A particularly good example of this was Memorial Bridge in Washington, D.C., where 44 percent of the daily volume in 1965 occurred during four of the morning peak-load hours.[25] If this volume of traffic were spread over six hours by having employees begin their eight-hour work day from 7 to 9 A.M., the average peak-hour load would fall by more than one-third, from 11 percent of the total volume to 7.3 percent. On expressways where the peak hour loads are a smaller proportion of total volumes, the advantages of staggering the work day are reduced.

There are indications that many urbanites are disenchanted with automobile transportation during rush hours; shifting their demand to public transportation will also reduce congestion. Table 7.3 shows the results of a *Fortune* magazine survey of automobile commuters in Los Angeles, San Francisco, and Washington D.C., which indicate that the modern city is not hopelessly wedded to the automobile. A majority of the respondents believed that some form of public transit system would solve the traffic problem better than would the construction of new roadways. In Los Angeles, the city most dominated by the automobile, 64 percent of the commuters said they would use a transit system if it could match their present driving time. Fewer than one in five commuters responded that they would not use a mass transit system under any circumstances. Imaginative and efficient public-transit systems would probably attract enough automobile commuters to reduce congestion without expanding highway capacity. Unless a peak-load pricing scheme raised the cost of automobile travel, public subsidies may be required to encourage commuters to use mass transit.

TABLE 7.3 **Survey of automobile commuters in three metropolitan areas (in percent)**

	Los Angeles	San Francisco	Washington, D.C.
Believe transportation and traffic problem in their area best solved by:			
New public rapid transit system	66	78	47
New highways and expressways	34	22	53
Type of transit system preferred:			
Bus system	35	21	41
Rail system	65	79	59
Would use transit system of choice:			
If round trip travel time matched present driving time	64	68	60
Only if it saved 10 or more minutes of travel time	19	18	22
Doubt use under any circumstances	17	14	18

SOURCE: Editors of *Fortune, The Exploding Metropolis* (Garden City, N.Y.: Doubleday & Co., 1958), pp. 79–80. Used by permission.

Urban mass transit can be based on bus or fixed rail systems, the latter being preferred by a clear majority of the commuters responding to the survey shown in Table 7.3. A rail system is capable of transporting large numbers of people along its routes at relatively high speeds. While a single-lane expressway can transport a maximum of 2,625 people per hour, an underground rail-transit system can move as many as 60,000 people per hour. This capacity, coupled with the high speeds made possible by technological advances, probably accounts for the commuters' preference for rail systems.

If a mass transit system is to be used effectively, it must operate close to capacity during the peak-load rush hours. This requires that many people travel between the high density central business district and other areas with large populations or collection points where commuters park their cars. Of course, few metropolitan areas have populations big enough to utilize the large capacity of underground rail-transit systems. New York City has over 800,000 persons leave its central business district each hour during the peak-load rush hours, while Chicago and Philadelphia, the nation's third and fourth largest cities, have volumes exceeding 200,000 and 150,000 respectively.[26] In Atlanta, a smaller metropolitan area with a population of 1.3 million (21st in rank), only 170,000 people are employed in the central city. This number, smaller than the volume of commuters leaving the CBD each hour in larger cities, is clearly inefficient to support high-capacity, underground rail-transit systems. In most metropolitan areas, the small number of commuters will support only mass transit systems based on lower-capacity surface modes, such as buses and nonexpress rail systems that carry in excess of 10,000 persons per hour.

If consumers prefer low-density urban developments and dislike high-density living, the viability of the CBD will, of course, be undermined and the advantages of a rail mass-transit system reduced. This problem is less acute with a bus transit system because buses cannot carry as many passengers as rail systems and are more flexible in the face of shifting travel demands. The principal disadvantage of a bus system is that it gets caught in the congestion caused by the private automobile, reducing the speed of bus travel and lowering its desirability relative to the more comfortable private automobile. This shortcoming, however, can be corrected if certain lanes of the highways are reserved for buses during the peak-load rush hours.

One respect in which the development of public transportation systems to combat congestion is superior to the expansion of highway capacity is that it does not homogenize the metropolitan area. High-performance public transit to the central city operates most efficiently along corridors of relatively dense population. The availability of high-performance public transit may relocate or concentrate dense activities, thus helping to create areas of high-density living—an economy of scale in consumption to metropolitan residents.[27] Some observers fail to appreciate this benefit, preferring to homogenize the metropolitan area by making the physical form of the central city consistent with modern automobile transportation.

> Manufacturing lofts, narrow streets and sidewalks, and other physical characteristics of older central business districts were determined by and suitable for a different set of technologies than seems optimal today. . . .
>
> A better longer term solution may lie, however, in adjusting the physical layouts of these older business areas to modern technological circumstances. . . . The major public policy for facilitating such changes has been, of course, urban renewal . . . it is reasonably clear that renewal does make a major contribution toward adjusting the physical characteristics of central urban areas so as to make them more compatible with modern transport and other technologies.[28]

To place a premium on the adaptability of a city to current manufacturing technology is to destroy the diversity of life style that offers consumers a richness of choice available only in large metropolitan areas. Furthermore, the advantages of homogenizing the central business district are modest if, as argued in Chapter 5, the technological obsolescence of the CBD has been exaggerated.

This case for a rapid transit alternative to the private automobile is based on the fact that different consumers may prefer different modes of transportation and life styles. Burton Weisbrod has argued that even those consumers who choose the automobile may be willing to pay something for the opportunity to use public transit sometime in the future. This demand for an option may lead consumers to be willing to pay for the service even if they never use it.

> Urban transit firms have come to recognize that persons who normally walk to work or use private automobiles will occasionally use public transportation, e.g., when weather is bad, or when the auto breaks down. These and other occasional users may patronize the transit system once or twice a year, or even less often. Yet an option demand will exist for the stand-by facilities.[29]

Users of automobiles may be willing to subsidize the provision of an alternative to the automobile in order to satisfy this demand for an option in case it is ever needed. For this reason as well as those given above, there would appear to be a strong case for a mass transit solution to the congestion problem whenever it is feasible.

Unfortunately, transportation policy is biased in favor of increasing highway capacity rather than expanding the public transit facilities. Because tax revenues generated by the automobile are spent only on highways, increasing motor vehicle traffic results in the construction of new highways. While local and state governments pay 10 cents of every dollar spent on expressways, they pay from one-third to one-half of all expenditures on mass transit. Although it is of dubious long-run value, highway construction is clearly the cheapest way for a city to increase the capacity of its transportation system. Ironically, current highway users can be made better off by allocating some of their automobile taxes to the construction of an improved public transportation system that reduces congestion and strengthens the viability of the traditional high-density central city.

Transportation and the upgrading function

The past two decades have been characterized by a dispersion of employment opportunities and an increasing concentration of poor households in the central city. Since public transportation from the central city to suburban job sites often does not exist, residents of the central city without sufficient income to purchase an automobile cannot reach places of potential employment. When public transportation is available, it is often costly in terms of both time and money.

If commuting costs are one dollar and one hour per day, a laborer works an hour longer for a dollar less, lowering a two-dollar wage for an eight-hour day to $1.66 per hour. By lowering the take-home wage rate, the opportunity cost of leisure is reduced. Given preferences between work and leisure, this lower price of leisure will encourage the worker to consume more leisure. Of course, this tendency may be offset by the response to lower income, i.e., the decline in income may increase work effort. The relative strengths of the income loss and leisure substitution effects determine the impact of inadequate transportation to job sites on the work effort of the central city poor.

Economist Oscar Ornati's investigation of transportation needs of the poor was based on the premise that "accessibility to place of employment, as perceived by a *job seeker,* is a determining factor of job-search and job-keeping patterns."[30] Even if a worker incorrectly assumes that transportation to a potential job site is expensive and time consuming, he is likely to believe the benefit of the search will not exceed the costs. Persons caught in the culture of poverty as described by Liebow in *Tally's Corner* may be discouraged when facing even modest transportation barriers. "In most cities the poor's accessibility via the public transportation network is thus handicapped more by lack of familiarity with the transportation network than by the absence of connecting routes."[31]

Increasing dispersion of employment opportunities into the suburban fringe makes it difficult to meet the transportation needs of the poor.

Low income may prohibit their use of an automobile, while the low volumes along any given route make public transportation expensive to operate. One possibility is to provide subsidies to the poor for automobile ownership. This subsidy has limited appeal since it both increases congestion and further reduces the demand for public transportation. Advantages of the automobile have been embodied into the public transportation systems with the "dial a bus" scheme. Small buses can provide door-to-door service between home and job at a cost per mile that is about 50 percent more than a private automobile but about one-fourth the cost of a taxi.[32]

A flexible and relatively inexpensive public transportation system would be of great advantage to the poor. The flexibility inherent in a dial-a-bus or similar scheme would greatly reduce the need for familiarity with the transportation network. To the extent that Ornati is correct in his assessment of the poor's perception of urban transit systems, the creation of such a program would be sufficient to meet the needs of the poor. Nevertheless, it is likely that unless free transportation were adopted, some poor persons would find the cost of mobility excessively high. Poor riders could be subsidized by having reduced fares for trips originating or ending in a poverty area. The appeal of this approach is limited by the fact that it reinforces the tendency to segregate families by income class.

Of course, the service may be inexpensive enough so that a generous guaranteed annual income would negate the need for special treatment for the poor. Although inadequacies in the urban transportation systems may complicate the lot of the poor, much more than improved mobility is needed to improve their socioeconomic status.

NOTES

[1] August Heckscher, "The City: Work of Art and Technology," in Brian J. C. Berry and Jack Meltzer, eds., *Goals of Urban America* (Englewood Cliffs, N.J.: Prentice-Hall, 1967), p. 20.

[2] Tabor R. Stone, *Beyond the Automobile* (Englewood Cliffs, N.J.: Prentice-Hall, 1971), pp. 2–3.

[3] Ezra J. Mishan, *The Costs of Economic Growth* (New York: Praeger, 1967), pp. 5–6.

[4] Denis Hayes, "Can We Bust the Highway Trust?" *Saturday Review*, June 5, 1971, p. 49.

[5] John R. Meyer, "Urban Transportation," in James Q. Wilson, ed., *The Metropolitan Enigma* (Cambridge: Harvard University Press, 1968), p. 49. Meyer also argues that some commuters may value their time in transit because it is the only time uninterrupted by wife or work supervisor. Such a situation is more appropriately used to question the sanity of the life pattern rather than to justify long-distance commuting patterns.

[6] Since terminal time spent in transit is not included, these figures underestimate the total duration of the work trip. Alan M. Voorhees and Associates, "Factors and Trends in Trip Lengths," *National Cooperative Highway Research Program Report #48* (McLean, Va.: Highway Research Board, 1968).

[7] Walter Y. Oi and Paul W. Shuldiner, *An Analysis of Urban Transportation Demands* (Evanston, Ill.: Northwestern University Press, 1962), p. 61.

[8] Jesse Buckhead and Alan K. Campbell, "Public Policy for Urban America," in H. Perloff and L. Wingo, eds., *Issues in Urban Economics* (Baltimore: Johns Hopkins Press, 1968), p. 600.

[9] J. R. Meyer, J. F. Kain, and M. Wohl, *The Urban Transportation Problem* (Cambridge: Harvard University Press, 1965), p. vi.

[10] This is emphasized by E. M. Hoover and R. Vernon, *Anatomy of a Metropolis* (Garden City, N.Y.: Doubleday, 1962), p. 102 ff.

[11] Hearings before the Subcommittee on Public Health and Welfare of the Committee on Interstate and Foreign Commerce, House of Representatives, 91st Congress, Serial No. 91–17 (Washington, D.C.: U.S. Government Printing Office, 1969), p. 25.

[12] Denis Hayes, op. cit., p. 48.

[13] For a discussion of this problem, see John K. Galbraith, *The New Industrial State* (Boston: Houghton Mifflin, 1967).

[14] C. W. Griffin, Jr., "Frontier Freedoms and Space Age Cities," *Saturday Review*, February 7, 1970, p. 17.

[15] Karl Moskowitz, "Living and Travel Patterns in Automobile Oriented Cities," in George M. Smerk, ed., *Readings in Urban Transportation* (Bloomington: Indiana University Press, 1968), pp. 151–152.

[16] Leon Moses and H. F. Williamson, "Value of Time, Choice of Mode," *Journal of Political Economy* 71 (June 1963): 247–264.

[17] For a rigorous presentation of this problem, see A. A. Walters, "The Theory and Measurement of Private and Social Costs of Highway Congestion," *Econometrica*, October 29, 1961, pp. 676–699.

[18] This proposition can be proven mathematically:

Let total cost (TC) equal average cost (AC) times the number of vehicles (q).

$$TC = ACq$$
$$\text{then } dTC = ACdq + ACq$$
$$\text{and } \frac{dTC}{dq} = Ac\left(1 + \frac{dAC}{AC}\frac{q}{dq}\right)$$

If the elasticity of average cost with respect to the number of vehicles ($dAC/AC \cdot q/dq$) is greater than zero, then the marginal social cost is greater than average cost (AC).

[19] William S. Vickney, "Pricing in Urban and Suburban Transport," *American Economic Review* 53 (May 1963): 452–465.

[20] Higher fees are likely to encourage private developers to create additional parking facilities. This possibility suggests that the municipal government must regulate all parking in the central city through control of either supply or price.

[21] D. Nichols, E. Smolensky, and T. N. Tideman, "Discrimination by Wasting Time in Merit Goods," *American Economic Review* 61 (June 1971): 312–313.

[22] Karl Moskowitz, op. cit., p. 156. It should be pointed out that 32.8 percent of downtown land is used for surface parking while almost half of the land is used for roadways and parking.

[23] Karl Moskowitz, "Tide Turns for Transit," in George M. Smerk, ed., *Readings in Urban Transportation*, p. 207.

[24] Anthony Downs, "The Law of Peak Hour Expressway Congestion," *Traffic Quarterly* 16 (July 1962): 393–409.

[25] J. Meyer, J. Kain, and M. Wohl, *The Urban Transportation Problem* (Cambridge: Harvard University Press, 1965), p. 70.

[26] John R. Meyer, "Knocking Down the Straw Men," *Challenge* 11 (December 1962): 10.

[27] John R. Meyer, "Urban Transportation," in James Q. Wilson, ed., *The Metropolitan Enigma* (Cambridge: Harvard University Press, 1968), p. 51.

[28] Ibid., p. 53.

[29] Burton A. Weisbrod, "Collective-Consumption Services of Individual-Consumption Goods," *Quarterly Journal of Economics*, August 1964, pp. 471–477.

[30] Oscar A. Ornati, *Transportation Needs of the Poor* (New York: Praeger, 1969), p. 3.

[31] Ibid., p. 12.

[32] Ibid., p. 88. Of course, such a scheme could also be used to reduce congestion on our highways.

RECOMMENDED READING

Downs, Anthony. "The Law of Peak Hour Expressway Congestion," *Traffic Quarterly* 16 (July 1962): 393–409.

Meyer, John R. "Knocking Down the Straw Men," *Challenge* 11 (December 1962): 7–10. Reprinted in D. W. Rasmussen and C. T. Haworth, eds., *The Modern City: A Book of Readings.* New York: Harper & Row, 1973.

Meyer, John R., John F. Kain, and Martin Wohl. *The Urban Transportation Problem.* Cambridge: Harvard University Press, 1965.

Moskowitz, Karl. "Living and Travel Patterns in Automobile Oriented Cities," in George M. Smerk, ed., *Readings in Urban Transportation.* Bloomington: Indiana University Press, 1968.

Ornati, Oscar A. *Transportation Needs of the Poor.* New York: Praeger, 1969.

Sherman, Roger. "A Private Ownership Bias in Transit Choice," *American Economic Review* 57 (December 1967): 1211–1217. Reprinted in Rasmussen and Haworth, op. cit.

Vickrey, William. "Pricing in Urban and Suburban Transport," *American Economic Review* 53 (May 1963): 452–465. Reprinted in Rasmussen and Haworth, op. cit.

Waters, L. Leslie. "Free Transit: A Way Out of Traffic Jams," *Business Horizons* 2 (Spring 1959): 104–109.

8
THE URBAN
PUBLIC SECTOR

Modern cities, characterized by complex interrelations between individual economic units, cannot be controlled by the self-regulating mechanism of laissez-faire that is basic to classical economic thought. Local governmental units play an important role in the effective operation of a metropolitan area. By providing sanitation facilities as well as police and fire protection, the urban public sector controls some of the negative externalities that can reduce the effectiveness and desirability of city life. Local government facilitates both externalities in production and economics of scale in consumption by making transportation investments that lower the cost of contact between individual economic units. Expenditures on education and public welfare are likely to influence the future employment opportunities of the young, making clear the public sector's responsibility for the effectiveness of the upgrading process in the city. There is no mistaking the important role of the public sector in the smooth operation of the metropolitan economy.

The scale of local government reflects its important role in the urban economy: In 1967 the 227 metropolitan areas in existence were administered by 20,702 local governmental units including 404 counties, 4,977 municipalities, 3,255 townships, 5,018 school districts and 7,049 "special districts." These jurisdictions employed more people than the federal government in civilian activities: 3.8 million workers with an annual payroll of $2.3 billion. The role of each level of government in the federal system of the United States is analyzed in the following section.

131

THE HIERARCHY OF GOVERNMENT RESPONSIBILITY

Economists specializing in public finance agree on three basic functions of the public sector. First, maintenance of full employment has been an explicit goal of public policy since the passage of the Employment Act of 1946. This category of public sector activity, called economic stabilization, has been a source of major concern since the Great Depression of the 1930s. Another function of the public sector is to change the distribution of income if the free market fails to distribute purchasing power in a socially satisfactory way. Finally, the government allocates resources in order to provide goods and services that the private sector does not adequately supply.

All activities of the public sector can be categorized into one of three hypothetical branches of government: the stabilization branch, the distribution branch, and the allocation branch.[1] Owing to the nature of these public sector activities, all are not performed at each level of government. The national scope of the federal government makes it most effective in fulfilling some obligations of the public sector, whereas in other instances, local government can best meet the particular needs of the population. There is an optimum hierarchy of governmental responsibility from a theoretical point of view. This hierarchy identifies those functions of government best performed at the federal level and those more appropriately met by local agencies.

Stabilization branch

Government stabilization activities are designed to maintain full employment of resources and relatively stable prices. Monetary and fiscal policy are the major tools used in the effort to maintain a high rate of employment without excessive inflation. Because the national government has control over the money supply, it alone can execute monetary policy. Fiscal policy changes the demand for goods and services by altering government expenditures and the income available for private consumption and investment. For example, if there is substantial unemployment, tax reductions and increased government spending might be used to increase aggregate demand. To satisfy this new demand, business firms would increase their output and employ some workers without jobs. Although judicious use of deficit finance might permit municipal governments to reduce taxes and increase spending in times of recession, local efforts at economic stabilization are unlikely to alleviate the pressures of cyclical unemployment.[2] Many regional economists claim that the economic well-being of a metropolitan area is determined by the demand of other regions for its output. Raising local demand, however, would not reduce unemployment in the industries that sell their output to other regions. To the extent that local economic well-being is determined by these "export" industries, economic conditions in a metropolitan area are influenced more by the state of the national economy than by local stabilization efforts. Local impotence to combat cyclical unemployment and inflation is not surprising in light of the high degree of interdependence among the individual economic units and geographic areas which characterizes a modern industrial economy.

Distribution branch

Ideally the distribution branch operates in such a way that a socially desirable income distribution is realized without altering the relative prices of goods and services in the private sector. This is accomplished by taxing some persons in order to increase the income of others. Although municipal governments have the capacity to tax some citizens for the purpose of increasing the economic welfare of individuals unable to work, serious efforts to redistribute income at the local level are likely to be exceedingly costly. If a local government chooses to improve the economic well-being of its impoverished households, poor families from other areas may migrate to the "pro-poor" municipality. Local control over income redistribution activities invites some governments to base their "antipoverty" program on sending the poor to more generous governmental units. As in the case of the stabilization branch, the high degree of interdependence in a modern industrial economy suggests that public efforts to redistribute income are best accomplished at the national level.

Allocation branch

If it is impossible to prohibit people from using a product or service for which they refuse to pay, the private sector will not produce it because profits cannot be made. Such a commodity is called a "social good," since if it is to be made available, it must be produced by the public sector. Providing these goods and services that cannot be produced by the private sector is the third function of government and is accomplished by the allocation branch. A classic example of a social good is national defense: If one person is safe from foreign invasion, all are. Public parks provide an example of a social want at the local level.

The allocation branch of government also supplies certain goods and services that can be profitably produced by the private sector. Public wants in this second category are called "merit wants," because the private market does not provide enough of the service to meet important needs of society. Education is a good example of a merit want. Since private schools teach students from kindergarten to postgraduate levels, it is clear that education is not a social want. General education is of vital interest to society—it is considered a cornerstone of a stable democratic system and fosters economic growth by teaching basic skills that increase worker productivity. Government allocates resources to education because, when left alone, the private sector would find it unprofitable to supply schooling to a great many low-income families. Since private education is beyond the means of these families, public schooling is required if they are to have an opportunity to improve their productivity and socioeconomic status. When the amount of a good or service provided by the private sector does not meet a pressing public need, it is a merit good that should be provided by the government.

Unlike the stabilization and distribution branches, allocation activities of the public sector need not be monopolized by the national government. A hierarchy of government responsibility for satisfying public wants can be determined by the geographic distribution of the benefits. If a public want can be satisfied at the local level with no significant benefits or costs spilling over into other areas, it should be provided by municipal governments. When a large portion of the national population receives benefits from the provision of a social or merit good, a higher level of government should provide it. The national government, for example, is clearly responsible for defense because the entire population is affected by national security.

The role of local government

These branches of government suggest which public services are best provided by local agencies and which are more adequately met by federal efforts. Table 8.1 shows a theoretical hierarchy of governmental responsibility for the provision of public services. Because there are virtually no public programs that are logically confined to state boundaries, the role of state government in the hierarchy is ignored. The very presence of state government complicates the administration of the 29 SMSAs that spread into more than one state, of which three include portions of three states. Residents of such areas are often more affected by policies in the metropolitan area of the neighboring state than they are by programs instituted elsewhere in their own state.[3] Metropolitan areas are the smallest geographical unit in the hierarchy presented here, because there are many government services provided by municipalities that influence residents of other jurisdictions in the same

TABLE 8.1 A theoretical hierarchy of governmental responsibility for the provision of selected public services

Metropolitan	Federal
Fire proptection	Education
Police protection	Aid to low-income groups
Parks and recreation	Communicable disease control
Public libraries	Research
Water supply	National defense
Sewerage and refuse disposal	Interurban transportation
Intraurban transportation	Economic stabilization
Urban planning and renewal	

metropolitan area. An analysis of political subdivisions within metropolitan areas is presented in a following section.

Discussion of the three branches of government suggests that the urban public sector should focus on allocation activities while leaving the distribution and stabilization functions to the federal government. If there are no significant economies of scale in their production, two criteria are used to determine which services shown in Table 8.1 should be provided by local governmental units. First, the benefits of the service must not spill outside the metropolitan area to a significant portion of the national population. Second, the functions provided by the urban public sector must not have a significant impact on the income distribution. Provision of city parks, for example, is a function that clearly meets both criteria for local responsibility. Disposing of sewerage and refuse is one local function that could affect the population of a wider geographic area, since a city that dumps raw sewerage into a river would make the residents of many cities downstream worse off. While the federal government need not provide for waste disposal, it may be necessary to enforce certain guidelines that prevent such undesirable spillover effects.

National government has the responsibility for stabilizing economic activity, for programs that have a major impact on income distribution, and for expenditures that may affect the well-being of the entire population. While the provision of national defense and some basic research are traditionally within the scope of federal activity, education is usually a local function in America. However, two aspects of the educational process suggest it should be financed by the federal government.

Because of the high degree of population mobility in a modern industrial society, it has already been argued that the federal government has primary responsibility for altering the distribution of income. An important aspect of education is the role it plays in the urban upgrading function. As pointed out in Chapter 3, acquiring education and training is the principal vehicle by which individuals can improve their economic well-being. Variations in educational opportunities between local areas will therefore influence the income distribution in the long run. Because it dominates the distribution activities of the public sector, the federal government must also have a major responsibility for the institutions that shape the income distribution.

A second justification for an active federal role in the financing of public education is that labor is a national resource. Economists often view the educational process as an investment in people, which raises their productivity and their contribution to society at large. Furthermore, educated workers are more flexible, adapting more easily when something forces either a change of job or respecification of a given task. Since few people in a technologically advanced society work at a single task for their entire lifetime, education is required if workers are to adjust to new techniques and remain productive members of society. If workers were idled and bitter because they could not adjust to technological change, national output would be lower and political stability threatened.

Many economists agree that local government is not well suited to provide educational facilities because the mobility of human resources generates spillovers or externalities from educational programs. In his study of educational spillovers, economist Burton Weisbrod concluded, "Mobility of the United States population is such that the vast majority of financial returns from public elementary and secondary schooling are generally realized outside the school districts which provided the child's education."[4] When making expenditure decisions, taxpayers in a community compare their expected benefits with the financial burden. In financing education, local taxpayers suffer most of the costs but only a portion of the benefits. Not wishing to subsidize residents of other communities, the taxpayers are likely to spend less on education than would be optimal for society at large. These spillovers have led a number of economists to argue that the federal government should guarantee for every citizen access to an adequate level of education.[5]

Federal financing of public education does not necessarily imply that local control of education must be forfeited. The national government might determine what level of expenditures per pupil is consistent with relatively equal opportunity, requirements for labor adaptability, and individual socialization. Compensatory funds for children from deprived backgrounds should also be included in this minimum level of expenditure per pupil. These funds could be turned over to local school districts with no direct controls above the accreditation procedures currently in force. Further, if residents of a school district wished to supplement the federal funds to improve the educational experience of their youth, they would be free to do so. Federal financing of education would help guarantee the amount and quality of education for every child and reduce the negative externalities fostered by inadequately financed schools.[6]

SPENDING BY LOCAL GOVERNMENT

Unfortunately the reality of public spending has little resemblance to the hierarchy of governmental responsibility proposed above. Public spending in metropolitan areas is shown for various categories in Table 8.2. Educational expenditures account for over $150 of the total $373 spent per capita for public services. When the $25 spent on income redistribution via public welfare is added to that figure, 47 percent of all local government resources were spent on activites that generate the most spillovers to other regions. In the central city portion of the 18 oldest major metropolitan areas, the proportion of direct general expenditures spent on welfare exceeds 10 percent, although there is an astounding variation in welfare expenditures per capita. In 1966–1967 New York City spent $89.30 per capita on welfare, over 18

TABLE 8.2 Local government expenditures within standard metropolitan statistical areas, 1966–1967 (amount per capita)

Activity	Direct general expenditure	Capital outlay	Total	Percentage of total
Education	$127.79	$22.56	$150.35	40.3
Public welfare	25.07		25.07	6.7
Highways and parking	11.32	9.82	21.14	5.7
Hospitals and health	15.92	1.28	17.20	4.6
Police protection and correction	19.33		19.33	5.2
Fire protection	9.77		9.77	2.6
Sanitation and sewerage	9.19	6.63	15.82	4.2
Parks, recreation and natural resources	6.92	4.42	11.34	3.0
Housing and urban renewal	3.68	6.08	9.76	2.6
Public administration	15.59		15.59	4.2
Utility expenditure	34.38		34.59	9.4
Other	32.69	10.36	43.05	11.5
Total	311.65	61.15	372.80	100.0

Source: U.S. Bureau of the Census, *1967 Census of Governments*, vol. 5 (Washington, D.C.: Government Printing Office), Table 9.

percent of the revenue generated from its own sources, while Minneapolis spent almost 20 percent of its own revenue for the same purpose. Among the more parsimonious cities are New Orleans ($0.94 per capita, 0.5 percent) and Saint Louis ($1.79 per capita, 1.8 percent).

These variations in welfare expenditures may be the cause of substantial spillover effects if the poor are attracted to the more generous metropolitan areas. However, differences in welfare expenditures between SMSAs may not be as important in generating these spillovers as is the inadequacy of welfare expenditures in small towns and rural areas. Because the national government does not guarantee even minimal financial support in depressed rural areas, many of these poor are forced to move to metropolitan areas. By this process, residents of major metropolitan areas are forced to pay a disproportionate amount of the nation's expenditures to help the poor.

A substantial portion of local resources is being devoted to services that are more legitimately functions of the federal government. The education and welfare burdens on local government, accounting for 47 percent of its expenditures, generate substantial externalities that affect the entire nation. These externalities should be "internalized" so those that benefit from the expenditures also contribute to their cost. Dramatically increasing the federal government's expenditures for education and welfare will improve the allocation of resources and relieve the fiscal problems faced by municipal governments.

MUNICIPAL REVENUES

Sources of local revenue within metropolitan areas are shown in Table 8.3. In 1966–1967 municipalities within SMSAs raised almost $363 per capita from many sources, generating locally 71 percent of their revenues, while the remainder came from states and the federal government. It is interesting to note that states contributed 26 percent of all municipal revenues while only 3 percent of the total funds available originated in Washington, D.C.

Local taxes account for $171 of the per capita revenues, or about 70 percent of the revenue generated within metropolitan areas. As shown in Table 8.3, the property tax accounts for $145 of this total, while sales and gross receipts taxes yield only $13 per capita. User charges account for 13 percent of the total and are the most important nontax source of locally generated revenue. Dominant features of these major sources of local revenue are analyzed below.

TABLE 8.3 Sources of local government revenue within standard metropolitan statistical areas, 1966–1967 (amount per capita)

Source	Amount		Percentage of total	
Intergovernmental	$105.55		29.1	
Federal		$ 10.72		3.0
State		94.83		26.1
Revenue from own sources	257.35		70.9	
Taxes				
Property		145.41		40.1
Sales and gross receipts		13.44		3.7
Income		6.75		1.9
Other		5.73		1.6
User charges		49.26		13.5
Utility		29.07		8.0
Other revenues		7.69		2.1
Total	362.90	362.90	100.0	100.0

SOURCE: *1967 Census of Governments*, vol. 5 (Washington, D.C.: Government Printing Office), Table 9.

User charges

Some economists, impressed with the efficiency of the market mechanism to allocate resources, suggest that the public sector should finance most of its services via user charges. User charges have great appeal when a service can be allocated by price and is used primarily by people who can afford to pay for it. Airports, water transport, and parking, for example, are facilities that are subsidized in a modest way by local government and are primarily used by relatively high income groups. Although the subsidy is a mere 87 cents per capita, it amounts to a total of over $111 million per year for all metropolitan areas. In the case of merit wants, imposing a user cost system would cause a lower-than-optimum quantity of public services to be produced because the ability to pay is not related to the universal need for the service. User costs are simply not feasible in the case of social wants, since users of the service cannot be separated from nonusers.

Economists generally assume that user prices can be employed to regulate the consumption of some public services in a socially desirable way, because the price of an item will influence the quantity consumed. User prices therefore provide a mechanism for regulating the use of public services. For example, if a central business district wishes to increase patronage of a mass transit system in order to relieve automobile congestion, it might increase downtown parking fees and subsidize public transportation. While user charges can play an important role in regulating the use of public services, they are not suitable for providing a major portion of the revenue required to finance the public sector.

Property tax

Levies on property account for almost 85 percent of tax revenues in metropolitan areas. Urban problems are aggravated in many ways by the numerous disadvantages of this tax, which grossed over $29 billion in 1969—about 3 percent of the gross national product. Property taxation is to a large extent a tax on housing. According to a 1967 budget study, a family of four with a moderate standard of living in a metropolitan area spends about $2,300 per year on housing.[7] Per capita property taxes of $145 shown in Table 8.3 suggest a family of four would pay a total tax of $580, a 25 percent tax on the consumption of housing! Being more burdensome to the poor than the rich, the tax is also highly regressive in its effect. As shown in Chapter 6, the poor pay a large portion of their income on this highly taxed commodity. This antipoor bias of the property tax is compounded by the federal income tax laws that permit property owners to deduct local tax payments from taxable income. High taxation of this necessary expenditure places a burden on the poor that frustrates the upgrading of lower-income groups.

Property taxes also discourage the use of land for public facilities, because development of such facilities raises municipal expenditures while reducing the tax base. Public housing projects, public buildings, parks, and roads erode the fiscal position of local governments. This problem contributes to the overall inelasticity of the property tax—it counteracts the miniscule increases in revenue resulting from a rising level of economic activity. Heavy reliance on the property tax thus raises the cost of satisfying social wants and contributes to the fiscal crisis that plagues many municipal governments.

A third shortcoming inherent in the property tax is that it discourages the improvement of real estate. When property is improved and its market value raised, taxes on the real estate rise. Costs of property improvement are therefore increased by the tax—a fact that may discourage both property maintenance and improvement. If improvements and rising property values are not taxed, the inelasticity of this tax is amplified and municipal revenues fall further behind the rising cost of public services. This defect in the property tax is particularly severe in the central city portion of metropolitan areas that have large tracts of deteriorating housing.

These shortcomings of the property tax have renewed interest in a modification called the *land tax,* originally proposed by Henry George late in the nineteenth century.[8] Because the land tax is not levied against improvements on land, and increases in the profitability of real estate caused by improvements are thus not taxed away, owners of real estate are encouraged to make the best use of their properties. Taxation of land is not a viable alternative to the property tax, because raising large amounts of revenue by this method would perpetuate the regressive tax on housing and the bias against public use of land. Urban problems will continue to be aggravated by the tax structure as long as the property tax is the primary source of revenue for local government.

Sales tax

Sales taxes are the other major source of local revenue. Like the property tax, this levy is regressive because the poor consume a larger portion of their income than do the wealthy. If food and housing are exempt from taxation, as they are in some areas, the poor pay relatively little tax. Eliminating the regressive features, however, greatly reduces the revenue-generating power of the sales tax. If equity considerations are taken into account, consumption taxes are not a viable alternative to the property tax as a major source of revenue.

THE FISCAL CRISIS

Unmet public needs abound in our major metropolitan areas. Inadequate waste disposal systems pollute water supplies, police forces are insufficient to halt the rising incidence of crime, and the central cities deteriorate for lack of funds to assist with their renewal. The Committee for Economic Development has estimated the fiscal future of state and local governments. The projections from 1965 to 1975 are summarized in Table 8.4 and show that the anticipated 82.4 percent increase in state and local government revenues falls far short of the 102.9 percent increase required for a constant rate of improvement in services. This rising deficit testifies to a growing fiscal crisis in the urban public sector. Future revenue requirements of municipal governments are determined by the rising demand for public services and the increases in the cost of producing them.

Demand for public services is often thought to be income elastic, that is, as their incomes rise people demand more of the services that are typically provided by local government. This demand hypothesis was first suggested by Adolf Wagner in the nineteenth century and is sometimes called Wagner's Law. This view suggests that cities will experi-

TABLE 8.4 Projected state and local finances, 1965–1975 (millions of dollars)

	1965	1975	Percentage change
State and local expenditures			
Constant rate of improvement[a]	72,056	146,226	102.9
High rate of improvement	72,056	154,519	114.4
Revenue from own sources			
Existing tax structure[b]	62,971	114,847	82.4
Expenditures minus revenues			
Constant rate of improvement[a]	9,085	31,379	
High rate of improvement	9,085	39,672	

[a] Projected 1965–1975 rate of improvement identical to the 1955–1965 rate.
[b] Tax structure of 1965.
SOURCE: Committee for Economic Development, *Fiscal Issues in the Future of Federalism*, supplementary paper no. 23 (May 1968), Part III.

ence a secular increase in the demand for their public services if per capita income continues to rise. Recent evidence, however, shows there is virtually no relationship between changes in state and local government employment and changes in per capita income.[9] Although hardly a conclusive rejection of Wagner's Law, this work does cast doubt on the conventional view that rising per capita income will increase the demand for urban public services and therefore aggravate the fiscal crisis.

An unrelenting rise in the costs of providing services is a major source of the fiscal crisis in the metropolitan public sector. William J. Baumol has argued that such a rise is inevitable because productivity-raising technological improvements are not easily applied to the activities of local government.[10] In the manufacturing sector of the economy, business firms frequently adopt many sorts of technological innovations that raise worker productivity. Because of these increases in output per worker, wages may rise with little or no increase in the cost of the product. By way of contrast, consider the technology of educational institutions operated by local government. Teacher productivity may be increased by raising the number of students in a class or by increased use of audiovisual instruction. Many observers feel that such increases in the student/teacher ratio, particularly at the elementary level, constitute a threat to the quality of education. If quality is diminished, the apparent increase of output may not in fact represent a rise in productivity. While worker productivity continually rises in the manufacturing sector, many areas of public employment experience only modest increases in output per worker.

As the productivity of manufacturing employees rises over time, the school system is faced with the option of either increasing teacher wages or permitting the workers in industry to earn significantly more than professional teachers. Ultimately, of course, salaries of teachers must rise to prevent them from seeking employment in the more technologically progressive sector of the economy. As public employees become more unionized, demands for wage equality between sectors of the economy will grow stronger. Urban services will cost more to produce because the rate of technological progress in the public sector lags behind the private sector. The dilemma is acute, for an apparent rise in productivity in the urban public sector may imply a decline in the quality of service. Our choice is clear: either more and more resources must be allocated to the technologically unprogressive activities of government or we must suffer a decline in the quality and quantity of public services consumed.

If the public sector remains relatively unprogressive technologically, local revenues will become increasingly inadequate compared to costs. A restructuring of local revenue sources is clearly required if spiraling costs are not to cause a substantial reduction in both the level and quality of public services. Shortcomings in property and sales taxes, which together account for over 90 percent of municipal tax revenues, make alternative sources imperative. The income tax is a logical alternative source of funds, for two reasons: It is not necessarily regressive, and economic growth automatically increases the tax base. Municipalities are turning more and more to the income tax; although revenues remain modest as a proportion of local tax revenues, they rose 500 percent from $254 million in 1960 to $1.3 billion in 1969.[11]

Federal revenue sharing

Federal government collection of a portion of municipal revenues is an alternative to the imposition of local income taxes. This guarantees a somewhat progressive tax structure, an obvious advantage in light of the fact that of the 47 cities over 50,000 with an income tax, only that of New York City and Washington, D.C., is progressive.[12] Furthermore, the federal income tax is an efficient tax in that it is relatively inexpensive to administer. There are two basic mechanisms for the transfer of funds from the national government to municipalities: general cash grants and specific grants.

General cash grants

General cash grants are federal transfers of funds to local government with no restrictions on their use. The Heller-Pechman revenue-sharing proposal is of this type, since the receiving government "would be given wider latitude—nearly complete freedom—in the use of their revenue shares."[13] If some federal taxes are automatically sent back to local governments, the national government would act as a collection agency for some local revenues. This would be preferable to a system that permitted the federal government to exercise discretionary control over the funds by offering grants to cities, because the uncertainty of grants would make long-run planning at the local level more difficult.

Specific grants

Unconditional revenue sharing may be inappropriate when the national interest requires that local areas provide adequate services. When funds transferred from the national to the local government must be used for a particular purpose, they are called *specific grants*. If the receiving government has no obligations to supplement the grant with its own resources, it is called an *unconditional specific grant*. Conditional specific grants require the local government to match national funds for the required purpose. For example, if the national interest required educational expenditures of $400 per pupil, the federal government could transfer $300 per pupil while calling on the local jurisdiction for the remainder. Specific grants are the logical mechanism by which the national government can assume financial responsibility for current local expenditures whose benefits spill over into other political jurisdictions.

When minimum service levels at the local level are in the national interest, specific grants from the national government are an appropriate way to relieve the pressure on local revenue sources. For education and welfare expenditures, unconditional specific grants from the federal government could guarantee an acceptable level of service for all citizens. Such a financing scheme would lower local revenue requirements by as much as 47 percent. Conditional specific grants might also be used by the national government to spur expenditures in areas of regional importance, such as control of air and water pollution. If all other local revenues were collected through the progressive federal income tax, general cash grants or revenue sharing would be the appropriate mechanism for transferring funds for the provision of local public services. There is no reason for any federal control over these expenditures, which are purely local in nature.

Such reforms would eliminate the disadvantages of property and sales taxes, revenues would automatically increase with economic growth, and all public sector activities could be administered by the appropriate level of government. Citizens could no longer avoid the cost of upgrading the poor by moving to suburban enclaves, since public efforts to reduce poverty would be paid out of federal tax revenues. Until the federal government assumes the financial responsibility for educational and welfare activities of local agencies, the urban fiscal crisis is not likely to be resolved.

FISCAL FRAGMENTATION: PREFERENCES OR FLIGHT?

The multitude of political jurisdictions in metropolitan areas has an enormous impact on the performance of the urban public sector. Metropolitan areas with a population exceeding a quarter million people were fragmented into 16,058 separate jurisdictions, an average of 137 per SMSA. Local jurisdictions include counties, municipalities, townships, school districts, and special districts that frequently administer activities affecting the entire metropolitan area. The Richmond and Norfolk-Portsmouth, Virginia, metropolitan areas are divided into seven local governments. Only six of the 117 large SMSAs have fewer than 20 political subdivisions, while 29 have more than 200. Philadelphia is fragmented into 876 jurisdictions, a poor second to metropolitan Chicago's 1,113 governments. The latter region has one "government" for every 6,300 people. Metropolitan areas smaller than 250,000 are less fragmented, although averaging a still impressive 38 jurisdictions per region.

If the quantity and quality of local services are determined by the users, a multitude of political jurisdictions can increase consumer well-being by offering more choice. Assuming consumer preferences for public goods are not homogeneous, people could satisfy their demands at lower cost when residing in a jurisdiction dominated by a population with tastes similar to their own. This view led Charles Tiebout to conclude that the fragmented local public sector is analogous to the private market:

> . . . moving or failing to move replaces the usual market test of willingness to buy a good and reveals the consumer voter's demand for public goods . . . each locality has a revenue and expenditure pattern that reflects the desires of its residents. . . . Spatial mobility provides the local public goods counterpart to the private market's shopping trip.[14]

Rather than seeking an optimum mix of public services, a less sympathetic view of multiple political jurisdictions argues that households seek to avoid tax burdens associated with the presence of poor residents. Poor families are unwelcome neighbors because they raise the cost of welfare and other public services while not paying enough taxes to cover the average per capita costs of education, parks, and other public goods. The presence of low-income groups raises the average tax burden required of relatively wealthy households for a given level of public services. All households therefore have a motive to isolate themselves from lower-income groups even if both populations have identical preferences for public services. While the existence of many political jurisdictions within a metropolitan area may foster consumer choice, the impetus for fiscal fragmentation more likely comes from a desire to minimize public service costs.

This interpretation suggests that the voter preference theory of local expenditures can be used to justify segregation by income class. A hypothetical example can illustrate the advantages of excluding lower-income groups from wealthy communities. If all households desire an identical bundle of public services costing $300 per capita, the $1,-200 burden for a family of four is 24 percent of a $5,000 income, 12 percent of a $10,000 income, and 6 percent of a $20,000 income. When families of four are willing to pay their $1,200 share of municipal expenses, there are no fiscal disadvantages to income integration.

When the ability to pay local taxes is related to family income, the disadvantages of income integration are clear. If, for example, the ability to pay local taxes is limited to 10 percent of income, a family of four earning $10,000 pays only $1,000 in taxes rather than the $1,200 required to supply the bundle of public services offered by the community. If a community is composed of an equal number of families with incomes of $20,000 and $10,000, the higher-income families must pay $1,400 in taxes or suffer a decline in the amount of public services consumed. If the community has equal proportions of families with incomes of $20,000 and $5,000 per year, the burden for high-income households is $1,900. Relatively low-income households are likely to consume more public services when residing in communities with wealthy families and the cost comparisons shown in Table 8.5 show that each income group benefits from excluding all households with less purchasing power. The large financial advantages of income segregation probably overwhelm differences in preferences for public services, indicating that the tax avoidance view is a more viable explanation of fiscal fragmentation than the traditional consumer-preference interpretation.[15]

An analysis of municipal expenditures within metropolitan areas lends credence to the theory that fiscal fragmentation is an attempt by upper-income groups to escape the fiscal burdens that result from the integration of various income classes within a community. Counties in which large central cities are located produce more revenue per capita than suburban areas but spend less on education and more on welfare and the protective services of police and fire departments. These rela-

TABLE 8.5 The impact of income integration on municipal tax burdens: a hypothetical example

Munici-pality	Composition by income level[a]	Required tax burden per family[b]		Maximum possible tax burden per family[c]		Total actual expenditure per family
		Percent of income	Dollars	Percent of income	Dollars	
1	20,000	6	1,200	7	1,400	1,200
	10,000	12	1,200	10	1,000	
2	20,000	6	1,200	9.5	1,900	1,200
	5,000	24	1,200	10	500	
3	10,000	12	1,200	10	1,000	750
	5,000	24	1,200	10	500	
4	20,000	6	1,200	6	1,200	1,200
5	10,000	12	1,200	10	1,000	1,000
6	5,000	24	1,200	10	500	500

[a] Municipalities 1 through 3 are assumed to contain an equal number of families from each income level. Each is a family of four, as are the families in other municipalities.
[b] Required for the optimum mix of public services, assumed to be $300 per capita.
[c] The maximum possible local tax burden is assumed to be 10 percent.

tionships are summarized in Table 8.6. By removing themselves from the relatively poor central city population, suburbanites are able to spend more on educating their children while reducing their total tax burden. This is possible because they avoid expenses generated by the large concentration of poor households in the aging central city. The very clear benefits of income class segregation suggests that fiscal fragmentation is a product of the desire to avoid supporting lower-income groups rather than variations in the demand for public services.

Local responsibility for financing services that affect the income distribution makes it advantageous to live in a community that excludes lower-income households. Fragmentation of a metropolitan area permits the children of wealthy families to enjoy a school system with high expenditures per pupil, while the poor are concentrated in culturally disadvantaged school systems that need extra funds to offer adequate compensatory education. Allowing local governments to influence the income distribution by variations in education and welfare expenditures denies a basic purpose of national government and frustrates the urban upgrading function.

ALTERNATIVES TO FISCAL FRAGMENTATION

The attempt of high-income families to enhance their socioeconomic status perpetuates the large number of political jurisdictions in most metropolitan areas. Fiscal fragmentation and local government financing of education and welfare make it possible for high-income groups to avoid responsibility for the poor. Upgrading the poor has not been a traditional responsibility of society at large because the American myth has it that wealth is earned through diligence and hard work, an opportunity available to all. Clearly such a view does not accurately

TABLE 8.6 Revenue and expenditure patterns in the central city and suburban counties of 15 major metropolitan areas, 1966–1967 (average dollars per capita)[a]

County	Revenue from own sources	Education	Welfare	Police and fire
Central city	300.48	118.65	33.52	39.31
Suburban	211.66	148.35	11.80	16.47
Ratio of central city to suburban	1.42	.80	2.84	2.39

[a] Similar although less dramatic results are obtained when all SMSAs over 250,000 are included.
SOURCE: U.S. Bureau of the Census, *1967 Census of Governments*, vol. 5 (Washington, D.C.: Government Printing Office, 1967), Table 12.

describe the reality of being poor in the modern city. Equal opportunity in a modern industrial society requires the equal access to educational opportunities, which is undermined by fiscal fragmentation.

One method of eliminating the multitude of political jurisdictions within metropolitan areas is to create a single government to administer the entire region. Such an approach has recently been adopted in the Nashville, Tennessee, and Jacksonville, Florida, metropolitan areas. Metropolitan consolidation removes much of the needless duplication of administrative activities inherent in fiscal fragmentation. Of course, reducing the cost of administration in this way forces all citizens to consume the same package of public services. To the extent that fiscal fragmentation is a product of the desire for consumer choice in the public sector, this is a disadvantage of consolidation.

Consolidation of municipal governments can also help bolster the declining fortunes of older central cities. With one government serving the entire metropolitan area, more funds would be available to preserve the central city because suburban areas have more taxable resources. Decay of the urban core is further reduced if, with tax avoidance no longer a viable reason for flight to the suburbs, middle class families are more willing to reside in the central city. Hence metropolitan government may play an important role in renewing the central city by forcing all residents to take financial responsibility for the entire area.

A major shortcoming of metropolitan government is that, like its fragmented predecessor, it must rely on an inadequate tax base. Consolidation does not eliminate the need for a local government claim on the resources that can be generated by the federal income tax. As already noted, the theory of public finance suggests that the national government should be responsible for basic educational and welfare expenditures. If the federal government were to finance education and welfare (activities that influence the distribution of income), metropolitan government could satisfy the demands for local public services.

NOTES

[1] The classic statement of this typology is found in Richard A. Musgrave, *The Theory of Public Finance* (New York: McGraw-Hill, 1959), ch. 1.

[2] It is important to distinguish between secular and cyclical unemployment. For smaller urban areas the decline of a major industry could cause long-term or secular unemployment. Locally initiated subsidies to attract industry may be successful in bringing new jobs to the region. The problem of secular unemployment is not typically found in major metropolitan areas. The above discussion focuses on stabilizing the business cycle, not on correcting problems associated with long-term changes in demand for industrial output.

[3] For a similar classification, see George F. Break, *Intergovernmental Fiscal Relations in the United States* (Washington, D.C.: Brookings Institute, 1967), p. 69. Although their boundaries are arbitrary, states may be useful for solving certain regional problems that are neither metropolitan nor national in scope.

[4] Burton A. Weisbrod, *External Benefits of Public Education* (pamphlet), Industrial Relations Section, Princeton University, 1964, p. 62. The same reasoning, of course, can be used to explain the federal responsibility for universal medical care.

[5] See, for example, Richard Ruggles, "The Federal Government and Federalism," in Walter W. Heller et al., *Revenue Sharing and the City* (Baltimore: Johns Hopkins Press, 1968), p. 70.

[6] Of course, money is not everything in education. For an interesting debate on the relative importance of expenditures per pupil and home environment, see James S. Coleman, *Equality of Educational Opportunity*, Office of Education, U.S. Department of Health, Education and Welfare (Washington, D.C.: Government Printing Office, 1966), and S. Bowles and H. Levin, "The Determinants of Scholastic Achievement—An Appraisal of Some Recent Evidence," *Journal of Human Resources* 3 (Winter 1968): 1–13.

[7] U.S. Bureau of the Census, *Statistical Abstract of the United States, 1969* (Washington, D.C.: Government Printing Office, 1969) p. 347.

[8] See, for example, Dick Netzer, *Economics and Urban Problems* (New York: Basic Books, 1970), ch. 7, and testimony by Mason Gaffney and A. M. Woodruff in the *National Commission on Urban Problems*, vol. 1, pp. 286–287.

[9] Bernard H. Booms and David Greytak, "Wagner's Law and the Growth of State and Local Government," Institute for Applied Urban Economics, Graduate School of Business, Indiana University, n.d.

[10] William J. Baumol, "Macroeconomics of Unbalanced Growth: An Anatomy of the Urban Crisis," *American Economic Review* 57 (June 1967): 415–426.

[11] Tax Foundation, Inc., *Facts and Figures on Government Finance, 1971*, p. 233.

[12] As of September 1, 1970. Ibid., p. 240.

[13] Walter W. Heller, "A Sympathetic Reappraisal of Revenue Sharing," in *Heller*, et al., op. cit., p. 7.

[14] Charles M. Tiebout, "A Pure Theory of Local Spending," *Journal of Political Economy* 64 (October 1956): 420–422.

[15] For a more sympathetic interpretation of the demand view, see Harry W. Richardson, *Regional Economics* (New York: Praeger, 1969), ch. 8.

RECOMMENDED READING

Baumol, W. J. "Macroeconomics of Unbalanced Growth: The Anatomy of Urban Crisis," *American Economic Review* 57 (June 1967): 415–426. Reprinted in D. W. Rasmussen and C. T. Haworth, eds., *The Modern City: A Book of Readings.* New York: Harper & Row, 1973.

Editors of *Fortune.* "Revenue Sharing is Not Enough," *Fortune,* February 1971, pp. 59–60. Reprinted in Rasmussen and Haworth, op. cit.

Heller, Walter, et al. *Revenue Sharing and the City.* Baltimore: Johns Hopkins Press, 1968.

Heller, Walter. "Should the Government Share Its Tax Take?" *Saturday Review,* March 22, 1969, pp. 26–29. Reprinted in Rasmussen and Haworth, op. cit.

Holtmann, A. G. "Migration to the Suburbs, Human Capital and City Income Tax Losses: A Case Study," *National Tax Journal,* vol. 21, pp. 326–331.

Long, Norton E. "The City as Reservation," *The Public Interest* 25 (Fall 1971): 22–38. Reprinted in Rasmussen and Haworth, op. cit.

Perloff, Harvey S. and Lowdon Wingo, Jr. *Issues in Urban Economics.* Baltimore: Johns Hopkins Press, 1968, Part III.

Weisbrod, Burton A. "Collective Consumption Aspects of Individual Consumption Goods," *The Quarterly Journal of Economics* 78 (August 1964): 471–477. Reprinted in Rasmussen and Haworth, op. cit.

Wood, R. C. *Fourteen Hundred Governments.* Cambridge: Harvard University Press, 1961.

9
CITY SIZE AND CONSUMER WELFARE

City size has an impact on the effectiveness with which an urban area provides externalities in production and economies of scale in consumption. Small metropolitan areas and relatively isolated urban places are not large enough to offer many advantages of agglomeration. Business firms in small urban places are likely to find a scant supply of business services and professional expertise. Consumers are denied special medical services and entertainment (such as high-quality restaurants, theaters, and professional athletics) because a small population does not generate enough demand to support them. Major metropolitan areas, on the other hand, have a population sufficient to support a wide variety of business and personal services. These advantages of urban agglomeration may be offset in our largest metropolitan areas by the problems associated with the interaction of large numbers of people. In this chapter the idea of optimum city size is explored and is then integrated into the concept of a hierarchy of city sizes—a concept that dominates much of regional economics.

IS THERE AN OPTIMUM CITY SIZE?

In this volume, urban areas have been viewed as factors of production, locational entities that society uses to increase human welfare. Existence of an optimum city size, of course, requires that the net benefits from agglomeration vary with the size of the urban place. It has already been noted that residents of large urban areas enjoy a higher level of

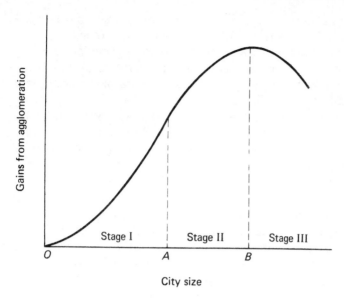

FIGURE 9.1   The relationship between city size and agglomeration
economies.

economic well-being because they can consume more business and
personal services than can inhabitants of small cities and towns.

The relationship between net gains from agglomeration and city size
may be similar to that of the total product curve commonly used in the
theory of the firm. Figure 9.1 shows this curve and three stages of urban
agglomeration. During the first stage (*OA*), the gains from agglomeration resulting from an increase in population are rising, i.e., the marginal
benefits are positive and increasing. Population increases continued to
yield positive benefits during Stage II (*AB*), although they are not as
large as in Stage I. The optimum city size, of course, is *OB*, where the
gains from agglomeration are greatest. Stage III may be called *dysfunctional urbanism*, because increasing population yields negative agglomeration effects. Beyond a population of *OB* in Figure 9.1, an increase
in population reduces the effectiveness of the city. Cities larger than
the optimum size do not provide as many externalities in production
and economies of scale in consumption, nor do they upgrade the poor
as effectively as a city with a population of the size *OB* in Figure 9.1.[1]

Stage I

Small urban and rural places that are not in proximity to metropolitan
areas offer few benefits of agglomeration, a shortcoming which limits

their economic and social viability. This conclusion is predicated on the assumption that workers generally change their geographical location if the economic opportunities offered by some competing location are sufficiently greater. Further, it is presumed that residents of these relatively isolated urban places have at least a rough idea of the economic opportunities in other locations.

It is generally believed that the economic opportunities offered by metropolitan areas exceed those of small urban places. For the most highly trained workers the relatively complete occupational structure of large urban areas offers a combination of more stimulating, prestigious, and higher-paid employment. If any opportunities exist for the professional in a small town, they are likely to be in professional services such as law and medicine. From a strictly financial point of view, the low level of income in small places makes them relatively unattractive locations for professional practice, because demand for these services is income elastic.[2] Persons desiring a career in management or business will also find their upward mobility severely limited by the absence of large regional or national corporations. Even the self-employed entrepreneur may find opportunities in a small town stifled by the lack of readily accessible professional assistance, capital availability, and business service. Hence, the most ambitious and able workers, those who could possibly increase the economic viability of the small town, are likely to be lured to larger cities.

Ordinary workers are also likely to find better economic opportunities in large cities, in part because most of the potential entrepreneurs abandon the small town. In addition to being driven out of small places owing to the lack of economic opportunity, workers with modest skills are also drawn by the higher wages offered by firms that can take advantage of the economies of scale made possible by a big city location. Furthermore, the combination of labor unions and oligopolistic and monopolistic industries in the larger cities results in higher wages than those offered by the competitive, labor-intensive industries (such as textiles and food processing) that dominate small places.[3] Because of the limited number of job opportunities, very small urban places do not facilitate the upgrading of unskilled workers.

It is reasonable to assume that the higher wage and greater occupational mobility characteristic of large urban areas will be reflected in differences in per capita income. In 1969 the incidence of poverty in nonmetropolitan areas was 17.1 percent, a figure 80 percent greater than the incidence in metropolitan areas.[4] In the same year per capita income in metropolitan areas was approximately 27 percent higher than the corresponding figure for the rest of the U.S.[5] Budget studies indicate that the cost of living is about 12 percent lower in nonmetropolitan areas than in SMSAs, suggesting that the real difference in per capita income between small places and metropolitan areas is about 13 percent.[6]

If we accept the initial assumption that workers are attracted to areas that offer higher wages, an exodus of labor from smaller towns would be anticipated. As experience has shown and as human capital theory has rationalized, younger and more educated workers are most likely to migrate.[7] Economic theory suggests that the marginal productivity and therefore the wages of the remaining workers will rise because they have more capital at their disposal. In this traditional framework, the rising wages should discourage further migration. This view, steeped in the tradition of the perfectly competitive market, is too simplistic and overestimates the viability of small places.

This automatic adjustment mechanism works only if there is enough new investment to keep the capital stock constant, so that it does not depreciate in the long run. Edgar M. Hoover's work on the location of economic activity suggests that most firms will locate either at the site of raw materials or at the final market—not at an intermediate site.[8] Since most small towns are neither significant final markets nor raw materials sites, they are relatively unattractive locations for new capital investment. Prospective employers may also be discouraged by the relatively unskilled pool of labor remaining after the highest quality workers have left the area in search of better opportunities.

If no new investment takes place in a small urban place, the decline in job opportunities is likely to accelerate over time. Demand for output falls as workers leave the area, further reducing the attractiveness of the town as a site for new business enterprises. This in turn forces more workers to leave the area, causing an accelerating decline in the amount of economic activity in the area. Location theory suggests that the long-run economic outlook is bleak for small urban and rural places isolated from metropolitan areas—unless these places contain growing communities.[9] Because survival is at stake, towns in Stage I reap great benefits from population increases that stimulate investment by business firms.

Underlying the dynamic decay of small places is the notion that the advanced technology of a modern industrial society and its accompanying economies of scale are inconsistent with the viability of small urban places as a location for productive activity. The trend toward greater metropolitanization of the population can be explained in terms of central place theory. Within this framework, an urban center supplies goods and services to its residents and also provides a central place function by supplying some items to inhabitants of "satellite" towns in the surrounding area. Small towns have the capacity to provide many daily items, but firms located there are unable to sell commodities that are infrequently demanded or that require large sales to achieve low costs. Larger cities provide smaller ones with the goods and services subject to these economies of scale. Central place theory is based on the premise that the market area of an urban place is its own population and that of its satellite towns and surrounding farms.

Because their market areas are dominated by farm families, the economic viability of very small urban places is declining. Since the farm population has declined from 23 million in 1950 to 9.7 million in 1970, demand for the services provided by small towns is falling. Slightly larger cities depend in part on the demand generated by these small towns to maintain their level of economic activity. Hence the reduced economic viability of small urban places is easily explained by the declining farm population, which reduces the demand for their output. In turn, slightly larger cities may experience a decline in economic activity as their market area shrinks.

The size of the smallest place that is viable in the long run is a crucial question for public policy. Long-term economic viability of an urban place depends on two conditions. First, it must be able to generate a level of real income and/or nonpecuniary advantages sufficiently close to that of metropolitan areas to prevent large-scale migration from taking place. Generally this will be accomplished by exporting goods and services to larger areas, since central place theory suggests that its market in smaller towns may be declining. However, it is likely that after a given standard of material comfort has been realized, the income differentials required to induce migration rise because of diseconomies associated with big city life, e.g., environmental pollution and congestion. Secondly, the smallest viable city must have sufficient size to offer an educational system that provides ample opportunity for upward occupational mobility.

While the U.S. population grew 13 percent between 1960 and 1970, Table 9.1 shows that almost 50 percent of all nonmetropolitan areas actually lost population. By contrast, all metropolitan areas have more economic and social vitality than nonmetropolitan areas, since only 15.9 percent of the smallest ones lost population. Using maintenance of population as a criterion for economic viability, there appear to be few gains beyond 500,000. However, there appear to be great advantages to population growth until a town achieves metropolitan status. Population size OA in Figure 9.1, which indicates the beginning of Stage II, would thus seem to be about 50,000.

Stage II

In Stage II the advantages of further agglomeration are reduced until the optimum city size (OB) is reached. It is frequently argued that the

TABLE 9.1 Population trends in metropolitan and nonmetropolitan areas, 1960–1970

Size	Number	Areas with population losses	
		Number	Percentage
1,000,000	34	1	2.9
500,000–999,999	38	1	2.6
200,000–499,999	83	6	7.2
50,000–199,999	94	15	15.9
Nonmetropolitan areas*a*	2619	1292	49.3

a All counties outside metropolitan areas in 1970.
SOURCE: U.S. Bureau of the Census, *Statistical Abstract of The United States, 1971,* and U.S. Bureau of the Census, *Advance Report PC (VI),* February 1971 (Washington, D.C.: Government Printing Office).

externalities in production offered by larger urban areas raise worker productivity and therefore the average wages. Table 9.2 shows that average hourly earnings for manufacturing workers are 12 percent higher in cities over 500,000 than in those under 200,000. Since the color, age, sex, and educational composition of the labor force vary only slightly by city size, these factors that influence worker productivity are not responsible for the positive relationship between earnings and city size.[10] In the area of worker earnings, it seems there are clear economies from agglomeration until a metropolitan area reaches a population of half a million.

Comparisons between the size of metropolitan areas and average hourly earnings in manufacturing are complicated inasmuch as industrial structure and the degree of unionization influence wages. For example, Detroit has the highest average wage of all the major metropolitan areas because workers are represented by a strong union in an area dominated by the oligopolistic automobile industry. Table 9.2 suggests that metropolitan areas exceeding 500,000 have a more favorable industrial structure than those under 200,000. Considering both city survival and average wages, the optimum city size would seem to be a half million or larger.

In comparing metropolitan areas, the advantages of agglomeration appear to reach a maximum (*OB* in Figure 9.1) at a population of 500,000. The data in Tables 9.1 and 9.2, however, do not give any indication that dysfunctional urbanism, a decline in urban effectiveness, sets in after this maximum is reached. Viewed from a strictly financial perspective, the rising cost of living that appears to accompany population growth is a potential source of dysfunctional urbanism that demands further investigation. If the cost of living is positively related to

TABLE 9.2 Earnings in manufacturing for metropolitan areas in the non-South,[a] 1970

Size	Average hourly wage median
Under 200,000	3.34
200,000–499,999	3.57
500,000–999,999	3.74
1–2 million	3.75
2–4 million	3.83
Over 4 million	3.74

[a] Many studies have shown that money wages are lower in the South than elsewhere in the nation. In order to avoid any regional influence in the comparison, southern cities are omitted.
SOURCE: U.S. Bureau of the Census, *Statistical Abstract of the United States, 1971*, Section 33 (Washington, D.C.: Government Printing Office, 1971), and U.S. Department of Labor, *Employment and Earnings*, vol. 18, no. 3 (October 1971).

city size, the constant money income for SMSAs of over a half million may, in fact, represent declining purchasing power.

Comparisons of the cost of living between metropolitan areas of different sizes cannot be made with the consumer price index.[11] Fortunately, the Bureau of Labor Statistics has developed family budgets for cities of different size for the purpose of comparing the cost of living between metropolitan areas. Although many factors influence the cost of living in urban areas, it is clear that budget costs rise with increasing population. Table 9.3 shows the cost of living for metropolitan areas of various size and indicates that it is over 5 percent more expensive to live in a metropolitan area larger than 4 million than in one with a population less than a million. This result is consistent with more systematic research investigating the relationship between cost of living and city size. One study shows that a 1-million increase in population raises the cost of living by 1 percent—after taking into account other factors affecting the cost of living.[12]

TABLE 9.3 Budget costs for metropolitan areas in the non-South, by size, 1970

Size	Average budget costs[a]	
	Cost in dollars	Cost index
Under 1 million	$10,559	100.00
1–2 million	10,805	102.32
2–4 million	11,071	104.84
Over 4 million	11,097	105.09

[a] Intermediate budget.
SOURCE: U.S. Bureau of the Census, *Statistical Abstract of the United States, 1971* (Washington, D.C.: Government Printing Office), p. 342.

Larger populations are likely to raise the cost of living in an urban area because they trigger increases in land rent. This can be demonstrated with the rent gradient model presented in Chapter 5. It will be recalled that the model assumes that all economic activity takes place in a relatively small geographic area, the central business district. The home-to-CBD trip therefore dominates the transportation pattern of all households.

It will be recalled that rent is a payment made to a property owner because his land is in an advantageous location. Inhabitants of a metropolitan area are willing to pay large rents for properties near the central business district in order to save transportation costs. If all commuters try to minimize the combined costs of land rent and transportation, competition for sites will ensure that the land rent for any site will equal the transportation costs saved by living there.

A rent gradient can be used to show how increasing population is likely to raise the cost of living in a metropolitan area. In Figure 9.2, the city population lives within OB distance from the CBD. An individual using land at a distance OA from the center of the city would be willing to pay a land rent equal to the travel costs he saves by not living on the edge of the metropolitan area (OB). Hence, the resident at OA will pay rent OR_1 which is equal to the time and money costs of travel from the urban fringe OB to the residence at distance OA. Of course, residents at the fringe of the urban area pay no rent.

An increase in population will tend to push the fringe areas further

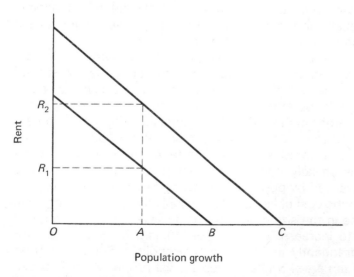

FIGURE 9.2. The relationship between population growth and land rent.

from the city center, say to OC in Figure 9.2. Transportation costs associated with living at the urban fringe are now increased, owing to the greater distance from the central city. Residents at distance OA now save more transportation costs than before (AC rather than AB) and will pay a correspondingly higher rent OR_2. If the new population did not push the residential limits further from the central business district, the population density at existing locations would have to increase. This could be accomplished by reducing the shelter space of residents, a reduction of housing quality that is in effect a rent increase. An alternative would be to increase the height of existing buildings, because adding more floors is a substitute for land in the production of shelter space. However, it has been shown that a rent increase is required in order to provide the incentive to construct higher buildings.[13] Increased transportation costs are therefore the principal mechanism by which population growth raises land rent.

Increasing population would raise the cost of housing for everyone in the city because of its effect on land rent. Since land is a factor of production in the provision of most goods and services, the cost of most commodities would also rise. For instance, after an increase in population, a dentist would pay more rent for his office; because his output would not increase with the rise in factor costs, his product cost would rise. Increasing housing costs require that the dentist raise his wage payment if he is to maintain his standard of living. Since the costs of other services (such as the barber) used by the dentist are rising, he must again raise his prices in order to avoid a decline in real income. Thus the costs of all goods and services are likely to rise to some extent when population increases in a metropolitan area.

Urban economists have traditionally argued that larger cities are more productive than smaller ones, owing to economies of scale.[14] From this perspective, one could argue that the increasing costs of land due to rising population are offset by the increasing efficiency made possible by the larger market. Positive externalities in production are therefore assumed to accompany any increment in population. Since wages do not appear to rise significantly after an SMSA reaches a half million, it seems unlikely that the productive efficiency of a city is significantly increased by population growing beyond that size.

An increase in the cost of living is not the only diseconomy stemming from an increase in the size of a metropolitan area. The incidence of crime appears to increase with city size. Violent crimes occur 188 percent more frequently in Standard Metropolitan Statistical Areas than in other urban areas, while crimes against property are 195 percent more numerous. The fact that violent crimes are 20 percent more numerous in suburban areas than in nonmetropolitan areas suggests that the lower socioeconomic status of central city residents is not the sole cause of the high crime rate in metropolitan areas.[15] This higher crime rate in larger cities reduces consumer welfare in three ways. First, merchants face higher insurance costs, which are translated into higher prices. Second, the tax burden may rise if additional police are employed to combat the increased crime. These two factors, of course, would be taken into account by the increased cost of living in larger cities. A third factor, the higher probability of being the victim of a violent crime, is an additional source of dysfunctional urbanism that accompanies large size.

Consumers in cities with rising populations will also bear increased nonmonetary costs as a result of the increased strain on the absorptive capacity of the environment. Air and water resources are capable of absorbing a limited amount of pollutants without impairing their quality. Because they are able to digest a limited amount of foreign materials, the discharge of some pollutants is not damaging to society. If the level of pollution exceeds the absorptive capacity of the environment, the quality of air and water resources will be impaired. Masses of people in large metropolitan areas are likely to threaten the quality of the environment with their air, water, and noise pollution. Congestion is also a problem associated with large cities. Since it causes more time to be wasted in nonproductive activities such as commuting, it is thus considered a cost of population growth.[16]

Optimum city size is usually defined in terms of maximizing the benefits of agglomeration rather than meeting the *demands* of consumers for city size. Many people will choose to live in urban places either larger or smaller than the optimum city size. For cosmopolitan urbanites New York may be the only city that could satisfy their desire for theater, restaurants, and other forms of entertainment. Such people desire to be in a place that offers great economies of scale in consumption; they are perfectly willing to endure congestion and sacrifice some efficiency in the production of goods and services to realize this end. Similarly, people who value ready access to nature and a nonindustrial environment wish to live in cities smaller than the optimum size. It would be irrational for such a household to live in an optimum-sized city, since it is willing to give up some of the benefits of urban life in favor of nonurban values. While the optimum city size is that which generates the most advantages from agglomeration, the inference that people should want to live in such a city may not be drawn unless they wish to maximize the net advantages of agglomeration.

Public policy should be guided by the wishes of consumers, not by the technical considerations that determine the optimum city size. If their welfare is to be maximized, consumers should enjoy a choice among alternative city sizes. Thus the distribution of city sizes is more relevant for public policy than is the optimum city size. In the following section, consumer preferences for city size are analyzed.

POPULATION DISTRIBUTION BY CITY SIZE

In the conventional wisdom of regional economics, the existence of an optimum city size is denied. For example, central place theory is based on the assumption that cities of different sizes perform different functions, normally related to the market area for various commodities.[17] Very small urban places distribute the goods and services needed by the rural hinterland, while commodities required infrequently are obtained in a higher-order central place that services many smaller urban centers. National centers, such as New York, Chicago, and San Francisco, are the highest order places where virtually all commodities and services can be purchased. Each level in this hierarchical scheme of urban places plays an important role in the economy. Recognizing that cities of different sizes are desirable and are optimum for some purpose, central place theory denies the existence of an optimum city size.

This approach to the optimal hierarchy of urban places puts complete emphasis on minimizing the costs of production. By implication, the distribution of cities that produces output at the lowest cost is the desired one. For example, if the costs of all production were lower in cities of greater than 1 million than any other location, the optimal distribution of cities would have a lower bound at 1 million. This geographic distribution of the population may produce a higher gross national product than others but would be highly inefficient if consumers *prefer* to live in places of less than 1 million! Increasing the alternative sizes of cities in different regions of the nation increases aggregate welfare by offering greater choice of residence to consumers.

The preferred city size distribution

Information about residential preferences is rather limited and of poor quality, although studies of different countries display a consistent pattern of preference for medium-sized cities.[18] For instance, Neutze noted that Australians found cities with a population of 200,000 to 1 million most attractive.[19] Niles Hansen reports that in France "70 percent of the Paris residents favor a diminution of the population of the Paris region: similarly, in other areas of heavy urban concentration, such as Flanders, the Artois, and the Lyon regions, there is also strong public support for a diminution of the population."[20] According to a 1968

Gallup Poll in the United States, a large percentage of the population (56 percent) indicated that if suitable employment were available, they would prefer to live in a small town or rural area. However, the responses to this poll are suspect, since the questions did not clearly distinguish between an isolated small town and a suburb of a large metropolitan area. A more reliable survey of preferences for city size has been conducted by the author and Charles T. Haworth. Respondents to the survey were asked to indicate the size of town or metropolitan area in which they would prefer to live if they could find satisfactory employment in that area. The concept of metropolitan area was explained, so that people would not choose a town of 10,000 when they desired residence in a suburban community within a large metropolitan area. Because familiarity with a particular size of place might influence locational preferences, respondents were asked to indicate the size of the city they considered to be their hometown. These questions were placed with examples of city size from 0 to 2000 (rural villages) to metropolitan areas the size of New York.

In order to get a range of home towns and various regional settings, the survey was administered to undergraduate and graduate students at Florida State University (Tallahassee), Temple University (Philadelphia), and Sacramento State College (California). Since almost 50 percent of all youth attend college for a period of time and because they have the fewest vested interests in a particular city, their choices may be a good barometer of the preferences of a large and growing portion of the population. While the applicability of the results to all segments of the population or age groups is not claimed, they are applicable to a large and growing group of people.

The locational preferences of 752 respondents are shown in Table 9.4. This table indicates the percentage of respondents preferring to live in the various size communities as well as the present distribution of the national population. It shows that the actual population is located in urban places larger than is preferred. While 24.8 percent of the population actually live in areas exceeding 2 million, the survey indicates that only 15.6 percent prefer such a residence.[21]

In their preferences for city size, consumers appear to have some notion about the optimum city size. Results of the survey shown in Table 9.4 indicate that the population is underrepresented in cities in Stage II, the sizes that reap benefits from continued urban growth. On the other hand, the survey suggests that many people living in nonmetropolitan areas would like to reside in a larger city and reap the great advantages of population growth that characterize Stage I in Figure 9.1. Metropolitan areas greater than 2 million are likely to be experiencing dysfunctional urbanism, and the sample suggests that 12 percent

TABLE 9.4 A comparison of actual and desired population distribution, 1970

Stage	City size	Preferred distribution (percentage)	Actual national distribution (percentage)	Preferred minus actual
I	0–50,000	24.6	32.2	− 8.6
II	50,000–99,999	11.3	1.0	+10.3
	100,000–249,999	6.6	7.0	− .4
	250,000–499,999	12.9	9.6	+ 3.3
	500,000–999,999	13.3	11.4	+ 1.9
		15.7	13.0	+ 2.7
III	1–2 million			
	2–4 million	5.3	7.6	− 2.3
	4–6 milion	6.1	4.5	− 1.6
	6–10 million	1.9	6.9	− 5.0
	10+ million	2.3	5.8	− 3.5

SOURCE: D. W. Rasmussen and C. T. Haworth, "Consumer Preferences and City Size," (mimeographed) (Tallahassee: Florida State University, 1971).

of the population residing in these large urban areas would prefer to live in smaller cities. This means that 25 million persons, the combined populations of the New York, Los Angeles–Long Beach, and Chicago metropolitan areas, would like to have the population of their metropolitan area reduced.

If the sample of college students accurately reflects locational preferences, the bias against large urban places is clear. Although 18 percent of the sample are from a metropolitan area greater than 4 million (compared to 17 percent for the nation as a whole), only 10 percent prefer to live in urban places that large. This anti-big-city bias may be based on the current conditions that have made "urban crisis" a popular description of our major metropolitan areas. Dramatic renewal of the central city of these areas might enhance their desirability as a place of residence. Of course, the preferences may also reflect the diseconomies of scale and negative externalities that are observed by many analysts of the urban scene. Under present circumstances it seems clear that many residents of our largest metropolitan areas would prefer to live in smaller places if suitable employment were available.

The need for a public policy that increases the number of people living in smaller cities is clear. While the need is great, our largest cities continue to grow. The population of New York grew 8 percent between 1960 and 1970, while Los Angeles and Chicago experienced increases in population of 16 and 12 percent respectively. Some of the forces responsible for this excess concentration of population in large cities, and possible corrective policy action, are discussed in the remainder of this chapter.

THE POLITICAL ECONOMY OF URBAN GROWTH

Attracting industry and people to an area has long been a popular goal of many private and governmental bodies. One need only glance through the pages of a business magazine to see the vast array of techniques and promotional devices used to attract industry and people. Even in areas without a significant number of unemployed, local public officials and community leaders have generally been enthusiastic supporters of "growth booster" activities. When unemployment is not a concern, two groups are the principal beneficiaries of urban expansion: landowners and developers, and certain "monopolists" who are not threatened by competition in either business or employment. By contrast, people providing easily duplicated services in highly competitive activities can only temporarily realize increased income.

Landowners

As noted in a previous section, population growth will cause an increase in the price of land in metropolitan areas. Such an increase represents a potential capital gain to all owners of real estate, the size of the benefit being determined by the location's accessibility to the CBD. This short-term gain will hold in the long run unless developments in transportation technology cause drastic reductions in the cost of urban travel. The typical homeowner with a single lot can realize this capital gain only if he sells his lot and moves to a location closer to the urban fringe where land prices are lower. Except for large-scale real estate speculators, the advantages of property appreciation are likely to be modest and partly dissipated by the tax increase associated with increased property value.

Noncompetitive positions

Industrial organization studies have shown that high barriers to entry are associated with higher profit rates.[22] Similarly, businesses that are local monopolies will reap the greatest benefits from urban population growth. In general, participants in any economic activity that is not readily expanded will stand to gain from growth, while those engaged in easily reproduced activities will not benefit.

Consider an area of 1,000,000 that experiences a rapid increase in population of 200,000. We note the effect of this change on two enterprises: a hamburger stand and the local newspaper. We assume there is one hamburger stand per 1,000 residents, each making normal profits. The rapid growth of population increases the level of business for each stand and increases its profitability. The higher rate of profit will attract new entries into this service until profits are driven back to their "normal" level and equilibrium is restored with one stand per thousand residents. Although short-run profits were increased, the typical hamburger-stand owner does not receive long-run benefits from an increase in population.

On account of the substantial barriers to entering the newspaper industry (e.g., economies of scale and capital requirements), the new population growth will not encourage the formation of another newspaper in the area.[23] With little change in costs, the revenue from both sales and advertising will increase. Thus, in the case of the local newspaper and other businesses that are relatively insulated from competition, profits are likely to rise as a consequence of population growth.

This phenomenon is not limited to those who own business enterprises that are "regional monopolies." Some occupations are "monopolies" in the sense that they are supervisory in nature and are not duplicated as responsibilities are increased. A comparison of the effects of population growth upon a classroom teacher and the superintendent of schools provides a good example. An increase in population will result in a corresponding increase in the number of teachers hired at the same wage rate because there are low barriers to entry into this profession.[24] By contrast there will continue to be one superintendent of schools in charge of more students, more teachers, and a higher budget. This increase in responsibility will be compensated by a rise in salary as well as assistants to handle the routine administrative tasks.[25] Those teachers or administrators who desire promotion to a more responsible position also benefit, since rapid growth of the school system will, for example, open up more principalships and deanships. To the extent that these are filled from within the organization, the ambitious individual has a higher probability of promotion in a growth situation than in a stagnant one. This analysis can be extended to any local organization in either the private or public sector that has a pyramid of authority.

The principal beneficiaries of population growth are those who have nonduplicable assets, such as land, or positions that are insulated from competition.[26] Growth also increases the probability of advancement for those who want higher-paid positions and are qualified for them. For those in duplicable positions, such as postmen, teachers,, and salesmen, as well as almost all employees in manufacturing, service, and retail occupations, there will be no significant long-term gains from population growth.

This analysis sheds light on the traditional American propensity to support enthusiastically efforts to increase urban population. Benefiting from growth are the wealthy, the inheritors of stategic land and property, and the most ambitious members of the community. Those engaged in the "opinion shaping" activities of television, newspapers, and radio communications, as well as public administration, also stand to benefit from population increases. The groups that gain from population growth have substantial influence on public policy and the community's acceptance of these measures. It is not surprising that public bodies in America spend millions of dollars each year promoting population growth, which may work to the detriment of the majority of the population.

In some areas community leaders have begun to question the value of continued population growth, suggesting that this coalition of self-serving community leaders is breaking down. The propriety of public expenditures for promotional activity has been questioned in Florida and California, and in other places concern about increased population has led public officials actively to discourage population growth. Governor Tom McCall of Oregon stated in 1970 on national television, "Come visit us again and again. This is a state of excitement. But for heaven's sake, don't come here to live." Similarly, the Colorado Environment Commission has taken the welcome mat from Denver's door. "Denver should have no more than 1.5 million people. . . . Suburban growth would be shut off by the establishment of a green belt of parks and agricultural projects 35 miles wide around the city. That would keep satellite communities from being established by people who could get into the Denver area."

Several factors may account for the increasing strength of the anti-growth forces. One is a clearer identification by the general public of the causal relation between increased population and environmental pollution. This is illustrated by the grand jury of San Bernardino County which recently criticized the county commission for spending $190,-615 in one year for national advertising to attract people and business and the accompanying pollution into that Southern California area. Smog conditions in the Los Angeles area have made air pollution a hazard to many people's health—and the grand jury's action illustrates this growing awareness by the general public.

A second factor that appears to be important is based on the notion that the traditional beneficiaries of urban growth are realizing smaller gains. The antigrowth forces may be led by gainers who no longer feel that the benefits of growth offset their own costs. This view rests on the assumption that the benefits for community leaders of adding 50,-000 people to an existing population of 100,000 are far greater than adding the same number to a metropolitan area of 2 million. Population increases in relatively small metropolitan areas will greatly enlarge the market basket from which consumers may choose—a substantial benefit to the relatively high income occupations that gain from growth. Expanding consumer choice is less noticeable when a city of 2 million experiences an increase in population because already available goods and services are duplicated. Further, the proportion of professional workers who stand to profit from growth is small in large cities. For example, medical personnel may wish to develop a specialized practice that requires a relatively large population but once this population has been reached, they have a diminished interest in growth.

A third factor, the law of diminishing marginal utility, suggests that the high level of income enjoyed by most gainers reduces the pleasure or utility of any increase in income. Declines in consumer welfare from pollution, congestion, and rising costs may dwarf the increase in income, even though net gains would be realized in strictly monetary terms. High income may lead many gainers to value improvements in their consumption role more than increments in their income. Urban decentralization is an alternative to continued population growth in existing metropolitan areas and is analyzed in the following section.

TOWARD A POLICY OF URBAN DECENTRALIZATION

In the United States the geographical distribution of population is affected by governmental actions that are conceived independently of a coherent population policy. Government decisions affect population distribution by such direct actions as the placement of educational facilities, transportation networks, military bases, and government offices, as well as by the indirect influences of import quotas, agricultural subsidies, and defense contracts to private business firms. These crucial government decisions are generally made without regard to their effect on the population distribution.

Consumer preferences and benefits from agglomeration in the production of goods and services must both enter into the analysis if a rational policy for the location of economic activity is to be realized. It has been shown that consumers are concentrated in metropolitan areas larger than they desire and that there are few if any gains in productivity due to population growth after the 1 million mark. Nevertheless, the population of metropolitan areas greater than 4 million continues to grow at a rate only slightly below the national population growth rate. This indicates the inappropriateness of the laissez-faire attitude toward city size and regional development that characterizes national policy. Consumer welfare and worker productivity might be increased if employment opportunities were more equally distributed among urban places of different sizes.

Local tax and investment subsidies are one way to encourage business firms to expand capacity in relatively small urban places rather than in our largest metropolitan areas. A municipality may reduce or eliminate local taxes for a new or expanding business firm, thus making it a more attractive location relative to other cities where production costs would be similar. Unfortunately, this approach to dispersion can be easily thwarted by similar promotional activities conducted by large metropolitan areas. Reliance on local subsidy programs fails to provide a coherent national policy for the geographic distribution of population and economic activity.

A national policy, of course, could be administered through the use of local subsidies if the federal government could offer local governments aid for promotional activities. Under such a scheme all urban places below a certain size (say, up to 250,000) would be eligible to receive funds to provide tax and investment subsidies used to attract industry. An alternative would be to allow tax credits in the federal corporate income tax for investments made in relatively small urban places. The size of the tax credit could be a function of the size of the urban area. For example, investments in plant and equipment in a rural place might receive a credit of 50 percent, while those in a place of 250,000 or more would receive none.

A policy that disperses economic opportunity and population may provide a desirable distribution of city sizes for a considerable period of time. However, the force of national population growth will decree a larger population for virtually all our metropolitan areas. Population growth may thus ultimately frustrate the purpose of dispersing economic activity and again force people to live in places larger than they prefer. The logic of the antigrowth position and individual locational preferences inevitably leads toward a policy of population control.

A policy that limits growth in urban areas is contrary to the American tradition of territorial expansion and the pursuit of economic development. If the emerging antigrowth coalition is based on declining benefits of growth and the diminishing marginal utility of money, the growth ethic that has been the cornerstone of both urban population and national economic growth policies may be undermined by its own success. If a more desirable distribution of city sizes is to be realized, it will be a product of a coherent public policy and not the result of natural market forces.

NOTES

[1] Some economists argue that negative externalities rarely offset the gains from agglomeration, even in the largest cities. These scholars deny the existence of Stage III. This position is analyzed later in this chapter.

[2] Milton Friedman and Simon Kuznets verified this in *Income from Independent Professional Practice* (New York: National Bureau of Economic Research, 1945), p. 221.

[3] This has been suggested by Wilbur Thompson and John M. Mattila in "Toward an Econometric Model of Urban Economic Development," in Perloff and Wingo, eds., *Issues in Urban Economics* (Baltimore: Johns Hopkins Press, 1968), p. 65.

[4] U.S. Bureau of the Census, *Statistical Abstract of the United States, 1971* (Washington, D.C.: Government Printing Office, 1971), p. 324.

[5] Ibid., p. 318.

[6] Ibid., p. 342.

[7] See, for example, Rashi Fein, "Educational Patterns in Southern Migration," *Southern Economic Journal* 32 (July 1965 Supplement): 106–124.

[8] The exceptions, called *footloose industries*, are generally engaged in intermediate stages of production. See Edgar M. Hoover, *The Location of Economic Activity* (New York: McGraw-Hill, 1948), ch. 3.

[9] E. M. Hoover presents a similar argument in *The Location of Economic Activity*, ch. 11.

[10] Victor R. Fuchs, "Differentials in Hourly Earnings by Region and City Size" National Bureau of Economic Research, Occasional Paper 101, 1967.

[11] Bureau of Labor Statistics Bulletin, 1570–5.

[12] Charles T. Haworth and David W. Rasmussen, "Determinants of Metropolitan Cost of Living Variations," (mimeographed) (Tallahassee: Florida State University, 1972).

[13] Charles T. Haworth and David W. Rasmussen, "A Note on Urban Land Values," *Land Economies*, May 1972, 196–197.

[14] For an empirical study, see William Alonso and Michael Fajans, "Cost of Living and Income by Urban Size," Department of City and Regional Planning, University of California, Berkeley, Working Paper 128, July 1970.

[15] *Department of Housing and Urban Development Statistical Yearbook, 1969* (Washington, D.C.: Government Printing Office), pp. 348–349.

[16] William Baumol has suggested that if every resident imposes congestion or pollution on every other resident in the city, these negative externalities will grow exponentially with population. See "Macroeconomics of Unbalanced Growth: An Anatomy of the Urban Crisis," *American Economic Review* 57 (June 1967): 415–426.

[17] For a brief exposition of this theory, see Hugh O. Nourse, *Regional Economics* (New York: McGraw-Hill, 1968), pp. 40–48.

[18] For a more extensive review and listing of these surveys, see Niles Hansen, "A Growth Center Strategy for the United States," *Review of Regional Studies*, Fall 1970, pp. 161–174.

[19] G. M. Neutze, *Economic Policy and the Size of Cities* (New York: Augustus Kelly, 1967).

[20] Niles Hansen, op. cit., p. 162.

[21] The sample was broken down by age, region, and hometown size to see if these factors influence preferences. Respondents from the Northeast, Southeast and Pacific Coast for each age category revealed the same preferences. Although geographical location did not influence community size preferences, hometown did make a difference. For instance, the median city size preferred by those from a hometown of 0 to 50,000 population was 100,000 to 200,000; while the median preferred size for those from a city of 4 to 6 million was 1 to 2 million.

[22] Joe S. Bain, *Barriers to New Competiton* (Cambridge: Harvard University Press, 1956).

[23] There are, of course, other potential barriers to entry. These include economies of scale in marketing or production, legal barriers such as patents, and limited access to strategic inputs.

[24] The average wage in a rapidly expanding school system may rise in the short run to attract additional teachers. The size of the short-term increase depends on the number of new positions. In recent years such a short-term increase in salary would not be anticipated because of the enlarged supply of teachers relative to the demand for their services.

[25] The superintendent of schools would support growth only if he were an "influence" or income maximizer. If he wished to maximize his leisure, he would view his increased responsibility as a source

of disutility. The nature of such administrative positions makes it unlikely that leisure maximizers would find them attractive.

[26] Henry George has been the most notable proponent of the effect of urban land rent (and therefore urban population growth) on income distribution. It is interesting to note that George's famous land tax proposal focuses on a special case of a more general phenomenon. See Henry George, *Progress and Poverty* (New York: Schalkenbach Foundation), 1948.

RECOMMENDED READING

Advisory Commission on Intergovernmental Relations. *Urban America and the Federal System*. Washington, D.C.: Government Printing Office, 1969. Reprinted in D. W. Rasmussen and C. T. Haworth, eds., *The Modern City: A Book of Readings*. New York: Harper & Row, 1973.

Advisory Commission on Intergovernmental Relations. *Urban and Rural America*. Washington, D.C.: Government Printing Office, 1968. · Reprinted in Rasmussen and Haworth, op. cit.

Fuchs, Victor R. *Differentials in Hourly Earnings by Region and City Size*. National Bureau of Economic Research, Occasional Paper 101, 1967.

Hansen, Niles M. "A Growth Center Strategy for the United States," *Review of Regional Studies*, Fall 1970, pp. 161–173. Reprinted in Rasmussen and Haworth, op. cit.

Sunquist, James L. "Where Shall They Live?" *Public Interest*, Winter 1970, pp. 88–100. Reprinted in Rasmussen and Haworth, op. cit.

10
THE URBAN FUTURE

Many critics of contemporary America claim that the urban crisis is a product of a distorted sense of priorities. They often argue that while spending billions of dollars on civilian and military aid to support governments with dubious democratic intentions, our cities deteriorate for lack of financial resources. Unfortunately, the rhetoric employed in debates on national priorities has often clouded rather than clarified the basic issues of public policy. In this chapter, urban problems are synthesized so that policy issues are clarified. The elements of policies required to relieve urban problems and the prospects for an urban life of high quality are discussed.

INTERPRETATIONS FOR PUBLIC POLICY

Traditional economic theory is based on the assumption that cataclysmic changes are not occurring in social phenomena. Thus, the state of affairs at any moment in time is a direct result of the individual actions and public policies that preceded it. Alfred Marshall, the father of modern price theory, sets the tone in his *Principles of Economics* with the epigram, "Nature takes no Leaps." This paradigm has led some to argue that the decay of major urban centers is a "natural" development stemming from the process of economic growth in America.

One popular interpretation of the urban crisis holds the efficiency of the American economy responsible for many of the ills that plague the modern city. Personal incomes rose rapidly during most of the twentieth century because of increasing industrialization. This rising per capita income, coupled with easier mortage credit, raised the demand for single family dwellings in the suburban ring. The flexibility of private automobile transportation made land accessible for low-density housing, and large numbers of people left their central city apartments for suburban dwellings. At the same time, rising productivity in agriculture forced many rural workers to the city in search of employment opportunities. These low-income families required inexpensive housing and found shelter in the apartments rejected by the new entrants to the middle class. Suburbanization of the middle class reinforced the dominance of the automobile, which, in turn, undermined the public transportation system. The central city became a respository for the poor and the suburbs a haven for the middle class.

This scenario suggests that the so-called urban crisis is merely a stage in the economic development of America. Just as it was natural for problems to arise, so will they naturally fade in the course of continued economic development. As the population becomes more urbanized, the stream of poor migrants to the great cities of America will diminish. At the same time, as rising affluence lures many families from the aging suburban developments, the poor will have access to large amounts of housing throughout the metropolitan area that will put them in proximity to suburban employment centers. Proximity of jobs and residences will improve the socioeconomic position of the poor, while a renewed central city will provide suitable housing for upper-income groups. Continued economic development may thus solve many of the urban problems related to the presence of the poor in the central city.

Advocates of this position can cite the continued decline in the number of poverty-stricken families in America as evidence of the healing power of economic growth. Both blacks and whites are becoming more affluent with the passing of each decade. In 1959 about 18.0 percent of all white persons in the nation were poor, while 54.6 percent of the black population shared their fate. By 1970 these proportions had shrunk to 9.5 and 32.3 percent respectively for whites and blacks. Further, the number of migrants from impoverished rural areas to the major metropolitan areas is also likely to decline. About 13 million persons left agricultural pursuits between 1950 and 1970, reducing the farm population to less than 5 percent of the nation's total. If the rural reservoir that has sent masses of poor to the city is drying up, rising affluence may eliminate many urban problems.

This interpretation of the urban crisis has great appeal because it finds the source of the problems in the success of the nation. Furthermore, under this interpretation the continued success of the American industrial machine and the affluence it brings will ultimately solve the urban crisis. It is essentially a conservative view that comforts a nation increasingly dismayed with the quality of life in its major cities. Continue on the current path, counsels the advocate of this position, for the natural development of the society will solve these temporary aberrations that seem so troublesome.

Although we are told that the thrust of America's industrial development will alleviate the urban crisis, there is a growing suspicion that to hope for such an easy solution is naïve. Confidence in the institutions that fostered America's development is lagging, while many of the myths that supported those institutions are rejected. The American experience with industrialization in the twentieth century has shaken our faith in the basic attitudes that transformed this country into the world's greatest industrial power. Policies and institutions that fostered the rapid industrialization of this country are not necessarily appropriate for a fully industrialized modern society.

The cornerstone of American industrialization was the free enterprise system, in which private business firms provided the thrust of the development effort. Individual initiative rather than government planning has been the American ideal in social organization. This system of economic organization may be socially desirable if effective competition rules the marketplace. Economists have long extolled the virtues of a perfectly competitive system and analyzed economic phenomena *as if* competition prevailed. Because the perfectly competitive economic model assumes complete knowledge and costless transactions, it ignores the importance of the externalities that characterize urban life. The reality of an interdependent industrial society has little in common with the traditional American image of a competitive world in which bold entrepreneurs serve their own and the social interest in the quest for profits. Continued faith in the individualistic ethic of perfect competition undermines our ability to solve urban problems that are the product of externalities.

Naïve faith in the market mechanism to allocate resources is clearly inappropriate in light of the abundance of market failures presented in this book. In housing, the Prisoner's Dilemma frustrates the maintenance and renewal of declining neighborhoods, even when the market rate of return from renewal is high if everyone improves his property. External effects also undermine the individual choices in the area of urban transportation, because with today's technology, pollution and congestion are the logical products of the decisions made by industry and consumers. The geographic distribution of the population is one of the clearest cases where private decisions lower the welfare of many citizens. Concentration of economic activity in larger metropolitan areas forces many people to live in cities far larger than they would prefer and is a product of the choices made by industry without regard for the interests of the population at large. Since private industry is ill equipped to consider these preferences of individuals or the external diseconomies it creates by its location decisions, it is a task of government that has been neglected by the public sector. This neglect has no doubt resulted from the traditional view of social organization in America that places great faith in unregulated private choice and is suspicious of the decisions made in the public interest by government.

The importance of poverty as an ingredient in the urban crisis is undeniable. Until recently the myth of Horatio Alger has been the cornerstone of antipoverty programs in America. The Social Darwinism of Herbert Spencer saw social progress as the result of competition in which only the fittest would survive. This doctrine, which deplored public attempts to equalize men's opportunities, received an enthusiastic response from the masses of Americans, reared to appreciate individualism and competition. Nothing but a person's ability and desire determined individual success. Captains of industry at the turn of this century raised a certain credibility about the myth, since some rose from poor but ambitious immigrants to command large personal fortunes. This myth has contributed to the urban crisis by making it unnecessary for society to design policy to equalize opportunity or to combat poverty.

The problems that plague our largest cities are a product of the interdependence of urban life. Public policies designed to correct deficiencies in a predominantly urban society cannot be successful if they are based on naïve, individualistic and competitive assumptions formed during the preindustrial frontier era. Because the traditional ways of looking at social phenomena in America are not adequate in a modern urban environment, a new foundation must be laid.

A SYNTHESIS OF URBAN PROBLEMS

Major urban centers in America are plagued by a bewildering array of problems that confound policy makers hoping to improve the quality of city life. When considering the problems of pollution, crime, congestion, poverty, central city decay, inadequate municipal revenues, poor housing, and the continuing sprawl of urban areas, it is not surprising that local and federal government workers are overwhelmed by their tasks. Unfortunately, separate analysis of each of these problems is not likely to yield effective public policy. If each issue is conceived as a problem independent of others, the common elements that provide the core of effective public policy will not be discovered. Rather than merely enumerate the problems, analysis must be conducted in such a way that potential solutions become apparent.

The complex problems of the modern city can be reduced to three basic shortcomings in urban life: an unequal distribution of income, the existence of negative externalities, and inadequate consumer choice. These issues suggest some of the policies required if urban problems are to be solved.

Unequal distribution of income

As we have already seen, one interpretation of the current urban crisis is that all the problems plaguing the city are a product of poverty in America. According to this view, the urban problem is essentially the poverty problem. Eradication of poverty would virtually eliminate substandard housing, arrest the flight of the middle class to the suburbs, and help revitalize the central city. While the elimination of poverty may not solve all the problems that torment urban dwellers, it is a clear prerequisite for improving the quality of life in our major metropolitan areas. In Chapter 8 it was argued that because of the great mobility of the American population, the federal government is the logical administrative unit to alter the income distribution. Hence the problems related to the unequal distribution of income are more the product of national failures than the result of shortcomings in the local administration of cities. As such, the solution to these problems must originate not from municipal governments but rather from a basic change in national priorities and policies.

Although concern for the plight of cities is great, the willingness to redistribute personal income in the United States is modest. Myths proclaiming the importance of individual self-sufficiency and initiative, which grew out of our frontier heritage, are slow to die in the face of modern reality. These traditional views undermine efforts to eradicate poverty. Among other things, America's intellectual heritage makes her ill equipped to correct the distribution of income and economic opportunity that is at the core of many urban problems.

Negative Externalities

The high degree of interdependence characterizing urban life fosters many undesirable side effects that reduce the welfare of residents. Some of these side effects result from the way in which we produce output in this country. Air and water pollution are major problems in urban areas, in part because private enterprise has generally been free to organize production with very few societal controls. As noted in the discussion of private automobile transportation in Chapter 7, pollution from that source is a direct result of the slowness of society to require pollution-free vehicles. Owing to the large scale of plant that characterizes many industries, firms produce for national rather than local markets. Local control of our large-scale national corporations is difficult, since the firms can move to regions that impose fewer restrictions on the methods of production and on product standards. Hence, some of the undesired spillover effects in urban areas can only be controlled by the federal government; their existence signifies a failure of national policy.

While pollution is primarily a product of national failures, congestion of transportation facilities is essentially a local problem. Local government can correct congestion by imposing peak load prices on users of transportation facilities or by expanding mass transit facilities relative to the use of private automobiles.[1] With the possible exception of some zoning ordinances, local governments have been as reluctant to control negative externalities as the federal government. At issue is the right of a property owner to use his resources in a way that affects other persons adversely. The laissez-faire tradition in America has been a slowly eroding barrier to our willingness to limit the individual's right to use private property in a manner that has antisocial side effects. As with the distribution of income, the American intellectual tradition and economic system are not attuned to the reality of modern urban life.

Inadequate consumer choice

The decline of the central city is partly a problem of inadequate consumer choice, a basic shortcoming in urban areas, which are supposed to provide economies of scale in consumption. Apparent preferences of most of the population for single family dwellings and automobile transportation have not only contributed to the decline of the central city but have also made it difficult for people with a preference for high-density living to exercise their choice of such an environment. Similarly, a large portion of good job opportunities are located in major metropolitan areas, while many people would prefer to live in small towns. It has been argued in this volume that the government should sometimes preserve the various options for consumers, even if the market does not indicate that *current* demand merits the continued production of the good or service. Burton Weisbrod has maintained that the national government should subsidize the existence of some national parks that cannot be supported out of current revenues because many people have a desire to visit the park at some future time.[2]

Because this desire is not registered in the market, revenue collections underestimate the true value of the park to society.

When aging central cities are renewed they could be rehabilitated as high-density areas, complete with the theaters, restaurants, and specialty shops that are presumed to thrive in such areas. An alternative is to make them compatible with manufacturing technology, so that the urban core is dominated by the low-density residences and automobile transportation that characterize the suburban ring. It is possible that the majority response in the private sector may lead society to eliminate the high-density central city that a significant minority of the population would desire to have. Thus the unregulated market choices, coupled with passive policy, permit such undesirable spillovers to exist. The inability of an unregulated market system to allocate resources in a highly interdependent urban economy requires the use of creative public policy to balance the desire for individual freedom with the reality of undesirable spillover effects that occur when individual choices are not constrained.

FOUNDATIONS FOR URBAN POLICY

It has been argued in this volume that some urban problems are a product of failures at the national level rather than shortcomings in the performance of local governments. If cities are to operate effectively to achieve externalities in production, economies of scale in consumption, and upgrading of the population, these shortcomings in national policy must be corrected. Even with far-reaching changes in national policy, the efficiency of local government must be enhanced if the highest possible quality of urban life is to be achieved. Reforms required of both national and local governments are discussed in this section.

National failures

In a modern industrial society, the contribution or marginal productivity of an individual is difficult to identify because of the great interdependence of factors in the production process. This ambiguity in determining a worker's "value" does not deter us from paying low wages to many people. One of the most dramatic failures of the national government is that it allows the market to thrust poverty on people who are willing and able to work. A man working full time all year at the minimum wage cannot keep a family of four out of poverty. The only fault of such workers is that their particular skills are not in high demand or, for some cultural or intellectual reason, they did not acquire the amounts or kind of education required in a modern economy such as ours. Widespread unemployment among highly educated aerospace workers in 1970 dramatized the individual's vulnerability to shifts in the demand for labor. Because of this feature of a modern economic system, it is imperative for the agencies concerned with the distribution of income to assure all individuals adequate income and employment. In Chapters 3 and 4 we saw that this could be accomplished through transfer payments to those individuals who could not work and a guaranteed job for those who are employable. Only the federal government can correct the distribution of income that is the source of many urban problems.

A second major failure of the national government is that it does not provide adequate methods of combating negative spillover effects. America's legal system is such that it places a premium on the rights of individuals who control property, guaranteeing a person the right to maximize the private benefit of his property so long as he doesn't threaten the property of others. Since some resources, such as air, cannot be assigned to individuals, they can be damaged with virtual impunity by the owners of private property. As a result, clean air and water resources must be protected to the same extent that the capital stock is protected from vandalism. These resources cannot be defended as private property because all individuals use them, and their ownership must be social. Unfortunately, the concept of individual property is far better developed in the law than is the idea of social property.

Private property rights in America must be altered if the control of negative externalities is to be effected. The essence of such a change in national law is that the ownership of private property would no longer be a justification for antisocial behavior. Freedom to use private property in such a way that it imposes costs on others must be limited. Such a change in policy could be a large step towards the correction of air and water pollution, congestion of highways, the demise of small urban areas, and the decline of the central city.

The legal structure must make it possible for federal and local agencies to insure that private property is not used against the public interest. Adam Smith, the father of modern economics, which is based on the strengths of the Invisible Hand in the marketplace, would not find this position repugnant. Smith had a great distrust for the businessman in the private sector and would advocate freedom of action for him only when it was constrained by the strength of a competitive market system. Only under such circumstances could the individual businessman be trusted to work in the social interest. In the modern city it is clear that the perfectly competitive system, which assumes independence of economic units, is not valid. We can only assume that Smith, as the intellectual father of the laissez-faire economic system, would advocate at least some controls over the use of private property.

Local government and urban problems

Correcting national failures that burden the efficient administration of metropolitan areas will not be sufficient to assure the smooth operation of our urban centers. Local leadership is often corrupt and lethargic. Part of this corruption is explained by the close relationship between local zoning activities and real estate interests. As noted in Chapter 9, large landowners and developers are likely to be active in the running of local government in order to assure that their interests are not harmed by land-use controls. Corruption from this source is reinforced by the low salaries typically paid by local government. Promising administrative talent can receive higher pay in the private sector; thus the city is often run by self-serving real estate interests or leaders of modest talent.

A major source of lethargy in local government administration is the paucity of resources at the disposal of local officials. Claims on revenues leave the municipal administration with little money to attempt innovative approaches to running the city. This shortage of funds makes it difficult for any administrator to make noticeable improvements in the performance of the city. Lethargy in local government may be a symptom of financial problems rather than a cause of ineffective local administration. The inability to marshal resources sufficient to support creative policy proposals may also discourage innovative administrators from careers in city government. Local government is often a political dead end that discourages some very able and ambitious people from basing their political futures on the sinking ship of metropolitan government. Creative and effective leadership is required on the local level if cities are to break out of the vicious cycle of urban decay and inefficiency.

Even the most dynamic leader on the urban scene is frustrated by the inability to effect areawide policy because of the multitude of political jurisdictions. Consolidation of metropolitan areas would greatly facilitate policies designed to make the city operate more effectively, since local administrations need control over the entire problem area if they are to be able to present effective solutions. A most dramatic example of the impact of fiscal fragmentation is the decline in the central city tax-base that accompanies the flight of the middle class from the urban core.

RESOURCES FOR URBAN DEVELOPMENT:
THE MYTH OF AFFLUENCE

Debate on the quality of American life often emphasizes the need for a reordering of our national priorities. It is claimed that if resources were reallocated, this affluent society could meet the pressing needs of our cities. A strange set of priorities for a nation facing a domestic crisis is revealed in the federal budget. In 1971 the federal government allocated over $76 billion to national defense and military assistance. This figure is more than twice the amount spent on agriculture, rural development, natural resources, education and manpower, health, community development, and housing. Many argue that an affluent society such as ours, with a painless reordering of priorities, could confront the urban crisis and greatly improve the quality of life in America.

Unless the 33 percent of federal expenditures allocated to defense is drastically reduced, it is unlikely that sufficient resources will soon be available to relieve the urban crisis. Affluence in America is often exaggerated. The U.S. Department of Labor has estimated that a family of four must earn $15,511 if it is to enjoy a higher standard of living in an urban area. This budget allows $11,346 for consumption—a comfortable but certainly not exorbitant standard—yet most Americans are far from this relatively affluent standard of living. Eighty percent of all families earned less than $14,460 in 1969. Fifty percent of all families earned less than $8,690 in that year, while the Department of Labor estimated that families living on incomes between $6,960 and $10,664 had a lower standard of living.

Most American families have a level of affluence that is not easily lowered by increased taxation. When 50 percent of all families live on what is officially determined to be a lower standard of living, it is not surprising that voters strike down many efforts at social and human development that would increase their tax burdens. Perpetuating the myth of affluence in America postpones the day when we will be able to marshal the resources to combat the urban crisis and improve the quality of life in America. Obtaining these resources will not be easy, for there are many competing desires among the majority of American people whose lower standard of living does not reflect an affluent society.

One way to lower political resistance to social policies that require additional resources is to reduce the number of people with a low standard of living. If the 1970 personal income per capita were distributed evenly among the population, each family of four would have $15,600—just enough to obtain the higher standard of living as defined by the Bureau of Labor Statistics. Given the value many Americans place on private consumption, it is not clear that even this wholesale redistribution of income would greatly enhance the resources put at the disposal of the public sector. The degree of affluence in the United States is not great enough to obviate the necessity of making hard choices between the quality of life and environment and the consumption of private goods and services. Given our proclivity for private consumption, it is possible America will choose to leave many urban problems unsolved.

THE MODERN CITY AND THE POSTINDUSTRIAL AGE

Most of this volume has concerned itself with the issues associated with making the large city a more effective instrument to improve human welfare. The issues have been primarily tangible—poverty, congestion, decline of the central city, fiscal fragmentation. They are tangible in the sense that they can be identified and quantified with a minimum amount of subjective evaluation. These objective problems are related to the way in which the city performs its basic functions of providing externalities in production, providing economies of scale in consumption, upgrading the population. Because of their tangible nature, these problems in the effective operation of the modern city can be reduced with the use of creative social policies and the application of sufficient resources.

There is a second type of problem, however, that is less easily identified but may be a primary determinant of the welfare of people in the future. In what is sometimes referred to as the "postindustrial age," the level of affluence may be such that supplying the necessities of life will no longer be a problem, and concern will shift to the quality of life. The essentially spiritual concerns over the quality of life are being discussed by increasing numbers of scholars examining the social fabric of America in the decade of the seventies.[3]

One theme that runs through this literature on what has been called the "counterculture" is disenchantment with the values and mores of the competitive economic system and the materialism that seems to accompany modern industrial development. Materialism in both capitalist and socialist countries in the western world is reflected in their almost singular appreciation for economic growth. These societies reinforce behavior that contributes to the economic growth of the nation, and people tend to keep their production and consumption as high as possible. The priorities are, of course, backward. Instead of people working to make the economic system grow, the system should be tailored to suit the interests of the populace. Critics of the modern industrial culture argue that rather than gaining more freedom as a result of their affluence, people are caught in the never ending race to acquire more goods and services, thus constantly acquiring new obligations.

Alienation may be an inherent by-product of successful industrialization. Edwin Dolan has argued that alienation is a product of industrial society per se rather than a particular form of social organization such as capitalism or socialism.[4] A principal force responsible for the alienation of people is the division of labor, which separates the workers from the act of creating a final product. Workers on an assembly line are virtually powerless to control either the pace of output or the quality of their product. Further, the lack of variety that typifies the efficient division of labor minimizes the amount of creative energy required of people on the job and undermines their vitality.

Although the mode of modern production may foster alienation among workers, American intellectuals have historically viewed the city with a jaundiced eye. In a letter to Benjamin Franklin, Thomas Jefferson wrote, "I view great cities as pestilential to the morals, the health and the liberties of man. True, they nourish some of the elegant arts, but the useful ones can thrive elsewhere, and less perfection in the others, with more health, virtue and freedom, would be my choice."[5] An antiurban thread has been traced through the work of an impressive list of American writers: Ralph Waldo Emerson, Henry David Thoreau, Herman Melville, Nathaniel Hawthorne, Edgar Allen Poe, Henry James and others. Raised in a predominantly rural society, many intellectuals in the formative years of America were dismayed at the individual anonymity and lack of community in major cities. As cities became larger and more industrialized, the validity of these criticisms became more apparent.

Jane Addams, founder of Hull House in Chicago and a leading figure in urban social work, shares this essentially antiurban orientation of many intellectuals of an earlier era. Hull House, according to Morton and Lucia White, was an effort to introduce a small-town feeling or a sense of community into the city. As an attempt to break down the impersonal big city, Jane Addams's Hull House is a monument to the unaffectionate attitude American intellectuals historically have had toward the city.

Alienation may be at the root of the anticity bias of many American intellectuals. This alienation may be a product of modern industrial organization, nurtured by the division of labor that gives men small and meaningless tasks. If alienation is inherent in modern industrial society, it cannot be removed by policy action. One can only succumb to the demands of the highly interdependent life of the city or retreat to a simpler way of life in the country. Perhaps Edward Banfield is correct in saying that the urban crisis is more like a cold than a cancer—the tangible problems of the city cause discomfort, not death; but the cancer of alienation may be impossible to cure. The literature on the counterculture, exemplified by Theodore Roszak's excellent *The Making of a Counter Culture* and Charles Reich's *The Greening of America*, are attempts to indicate new directions for life in a modern industrial society. To no small extent they represent individual efforts to carve out a meaningful life within the essentially alienating framework of modern industrial society. Formal social structures in a modern industrial society may be ill equipped to reduce the level of subjective alienation inherent in such a society. The lessons of the counterculture are much like those of other essentially religious influences concerned with the quality of the individual's life: The social structure can solve only the easier problems of tangible shortcomings; the individual is the sole component of society capable of working toward a satisfying life.

NOTES

[1] Of course, by requiring that all automobile taxes be spent on highways, the federal government discourages expansion of mass transit facilities.

[2] Burton A. Weisbrod, "Collective Aspects of Individual Consumption Goods," *Quarterly Journal of Economics* 78 (August 1964): 471–477.

[3] See Theodore Roszak, ed., *Sources: An Anthology of Contemporary Materials Useful For Preserving Personal Sanity While Braving the Great Technological Wilderness* (New York: Harper & Row, 1972).

[4] Edwin C. Dolan, "Alienation, Freedom and Economic Organization," *Journal of Political Economy* 79 (September/October 1971): 1084–1094.

[5] Morton and Lucia White, *The Intellectual Versus the City* (Cambridge: Harvard University Press, 1962), p. 17.

INDEX

73 74 75 76 9 8 7 6 5 4 3 2 1